The Culture of Stopping

For Nicholas Czichi-Welzer

The Culture of Stopping
Obituary to Myself

HARALD WELZER

Translated by Sharon Howe

polity

Originally published in German as *Nachruf auf mich selbst. Die Kultur des Aufhörens*
Copyright © 2021 S. Fischer Verlag GmbH, Frankfurt am Main.

This English edition © Polity Press, 2023

Polity Press
65 Bridge Street
Cambridge CB2 1UR, UK

Polity Press
111 River Street
Hoboken, NJ 07030, USA

ISBN-13: 978-1-5095-5587-1- hardback

A catalogue record for this book is available from the British Library.

Library of Congress Control Number: 2022948602

Typeset in 11 on 14pt Warnock Pro
by Cheshire Typesetting Ltd, Cuddington, Cheshire
Printed and bound in the UK by CPI Group (UK) Ltd, Croydon

The publisher has used its best endeavours to ensure that the URLs for external websites referred to in this book are correct and active at the time of going to press. However, the publisher has no responsibility for the websites and can make no guarantee that a site will remain live or that the content is or will remain appropriate.

Every effort has been made to trace all copyright holders, but if any have been overlooked the publisher will be pleased to include any necessary credits in any subsequent reprint or edition.

For further information on Polity, visit our website: politybooks.com

Contents

Acknowledgements

I learnt a great deal from a number of people while working on this book: from Reinhold Messner, Johannes Heimrath, Katja Baumgarten, Christiane zu Salm, Thomas Kessler, Hans-Dietrich Reckhaus, Peter Sillem, Klaus Wiegandt – for that, and for your time and input, I am truly grateful to you all. Jochen Hein and Hans Ulrich Gruber were extremely helpful and contributed photos and information – my thanks to you both and I hope to see you again soon! The writing of this book coincided with various lockdowns, resulting in long evenings on Zoom which were partly spent tossing around ideas for this book – my heartfelt thanks to Siegrun Appelt, Heidi Borhau and Alexander Roesler for listening and contributing your thoughts and inspiration.

Finally, a very special thank you to Sonja Diekmann for making this book possible in the first place by ensuring that the author is still alive and kicking today.

Berlin, July 2021

Illustrations

I

Away from Here

I gave orders for my horse to be brought from the stables. The servant did not understand my orders. So I went to the stable myself, saddled my horse and mounted. In the distance I heard the sound of a trumpet, and I asked the servant what this meant. He knew nothing and had heard nothing. At the gate he stopped me, asking: 'Where are you riding to, master?' 'I don't know,' I said, 'just away from here, just away from here. Further and further away from here, only then can I reach my destination.' 'And so you know your destination?' he asked. 'Yes,' I replied, 'I've just told you. Away-from-here, that is my destination.'

Franz Kafka, 'The Departure'

Dead mass and life

The mass of man-made objects has doubled approximately every 20 years since 1900. At that time, it was equivalent to around 3 per cent of biomass: that is, 3 per cent of all living matter. In 2020, dead mass – houses, asphalt, machinery, cars, plastic, computers and the like – exceeded biomass for the first time. By contrast, the biomass of all wildlife has shrunk by more than four-fifths over the past 50 years. This is a staggering development. According to scientists at the Israeli Weizmann Institute,[1] while biomass continues to diminish due to deforestation, soil and ocean degradation and species extinction, the mass of man-made objects is growing faster than ever.

To help visualize this process, it has been calculated that the amount of stuff produced each week is equivalent to the body weight of every person on earth. That's fifty-two times a year that your own weight in dead mass is added to the total. It all sounds a bit creepy to me, although I should stress that this fifty-two-times-me figure consists of substances taken from the living soils, forests, oceans and rivers – indeed, where else would they come from? In other words, the world is being converted at an ever-faster rate from a natural one to an artificial one or, rather, from a living one to a dead one. A victory of man-made products over biomass. Of dead stuff over living stuff.

On 23 March 2021, something happened that brought this fact directly to our television screens: the 400-metre-long and almost 60-metre-wide container ship *Ever Given* became stuck – quite literally – in the Suez Canal. Opened in 1869, this waterway was never designed for a vessel of such monumental proportions, and the incident brought a large part of the world's freight traffic to a standstill. In no time, another 150 cargo ships were queuing up on either side of the canal, in the Mediterranean and Red Sea. The costs incurred by such a snarl-up are enormous, as the punctual delivery of the cargoes can no longer be guaranteed by a global supply chain based on just-in-time logistics. In this case, chemical, automotive and electronics manufacturers waited in desperation for the monster ship to free itself. But all to no avail. Because in addition to its dead weight of 220,000 tons, it was also carrying over 20,000 containers, and once something of that size has run aground, it's no easy feat to dislodge it.

Fig. 1.1:   The *Ever Given*, stuck fast

As if to highlight the absurdity of our way of life and economic system, the ship in question gloried in the name *Ever Given*. And just as that huge vessel found itself stuck helplessly in limbo, so our cultural model seems helplessly stuck between past and future.

The radically accelerated conversion of matter is fast consuming the very resources it depends on: at some point, this 'ever given' too will run aground. I have just read a piece by the anthropologist Michael Tomasello in which he argues that human culture has led to the fascinating co-evolutionary principle of cultural inheritance. Every new human child is born into a world where it can build on the achievements of its predecessors' cultural evolution. Tomasello calls this the 'ratchet effect' of the human condition: a new generation never starts from scratch but always from the point where the previous one left off. This is what distinguishes human life from that of all other living creatures. It is co-evolutionary: humans don't only exist in a natural environment but also in one of their own making. This is what we call culture.

The question Tomasello fails to ask himself is this: what if our cultural development has taken a wrong turn – one that is detrimental to our survival? That process then continues for a few more generations and, since the world each of those generations is born into is the only one they know, it inevitably takes time for anyone to notice that the direction of travel is unsustainable. For the culture we grow into is not something external – it is not only embedded in our infrastructures and institutions, our legal constitution, our school curricula and our traffic regulations, but in our habits, our perceptions and interpretations, our psyche, our selves. Just as we shape our way of life, so we are shaped by it, and that shaping is not conscious and intentional but a product of our everyday practices.

Practices like the expectation in modern hyper-consumerist societies that we can have anything we want, whenever we want it. This is something we take completely for granted, and it's only when 'shortages' occur due to disasters like the Suez Canal incident that we realize that all the stuff in our shopping precincts doesn't appear by magic but actually comes from somewhere. How it got there is a question our cultural model systematically ignores. This is the 'cultural unconscious', and, as members of this culture, we are all practised in the art of forgetting. When we get our hands on a nice new iPhone, we're not the least bit interested in its manifold and complex origins. So accustomed are we to constant availability, it doesn't even occur to us to ask ourselves this question.

To take another example: just as economic performance is measured in quantitative terms and expressed in exchange rates and GDP, so the need to measure things has permeated almost every aspect of our lives – from school grades and credit points to the number of dates we've been on, or our daily step count. The iPhone, Apple Watch and Peloton body-control apps are a prime illustration of how numbers have become an everyday part not just of the way we present but also the way we perceive ourselves. This migration of the quantitative into our inner selves and our mental landscape clearly shows that culture is never something external, surrounding human beings like environmental furniture, but always translates itself into the inner worlds of our psyche and sense of self-worth. And because culture changes, we will always be different from our predecessors, right down to our sensory perceptions, emotions and self-image.

This is what makes it so difficult to imagine that the culture one belongs to could be heading in the 'wrong' direction. After all, that culture has always been 'there' for all of us, like water around a fish. But it is perhaps fair to say that a culture that consumes the very basis of its existence is, at the very least, misguided. Nor would this be anything new in the context of human history. We have seen cultures of mass murder, delusional cultures, and cultures that have dumped their baggage on places where it didn't belong. And we have seen cultures that have pursued a path leading to disaster and self-destruction.

In his important book on failed cultures, *Collapse*, Jared Diamond has argued that what appears as a mistake when reconstructed historically is not perceived as such by people at the time but simply as the way things have always been done. After all, deforestation, soil erosion, salinization, overhunting and overfishing, population growth and rising wealth[2] have no time index from an individual perspective. Our perception changes with our changing environment, and the alarming realization that we are on the wrong track only comes in retrospect, if at all. Normally, we are swept along on the tide of change, by which time we no longer have any fixed reference points from which to judge what has changed and when things started going awry. Such 'shifting baselines'[3] consistently prevent us from recognizing an ongoing decline or actual failure, which is why such an epochal event as the collapse of the entire Eastern bloc, including the GDR, in 1989 was not predicted even by any of the relevant disciplines – history, political science, sociology or economics – but appeared to happen just like that, out of the blue. Oops.

So if we ask ourselves questions like 'What was the man who cut down the last palm tree on Easter Island thinking?', 'What were the Greenland Vikings thinking when they wasted their resources on trying to farm cattle in Arctic conditions?', 'What were engineers in the age of climate change thinking when they designed gas-guzzling 4 × 4s for city dwellers?', then the answer in each case is nothing: they weren't thinking at all. Because all these things are the product of long-term developments that become established cultural practice. And all new arrivals are simply absorbed into the flow – just as children today are born into a world of cars and computer screens. Tomasello's ratchet effect operates regardless of whether or not the evolving culture is conducive to our long-term survival. Where trees have always been felled, they will go on being felled.

Cultural practice is lived practice, not a matter of discussion, reflection or thought, where you can simply say: hang on, something's not right here! And that is why such practices persist, sometimes even at the risk of damaging personal interests. To apply this to today's economic system: we keep on raising production because that's what we have always done – a fall in GDP is considered a disaster to be avoided at all costs. When the COVID crisis hit, economists didn't have a clue how to tackle it, yet they managed to calculate in a flash – and to the last decimal place – that the economy would grow by such-and-such a percentage in the fourth quarter of 2020. And by such-and-such a percentage in 2021. Their forecast was wrong – as usual – but the funny thing is, it doesn't matter. Standard economics sees itself as a science and is regarded as such by society, yet it is, at bottom, a priesthood. It has its own ceremonial proclamations (of decisions reached by the economic sages), pilgrimages (to the World Economic Forum in Davos) and magical explanations for the world order (the market moves in mysterious ways), no different from the priests of Easter Island. And its god is called Growth.

It could be that this principle of growth-based capitalism belongs to the category of failed cultural models. And this is of course all the harder to grasp since capitalism has brought such concrete improvements in education, health, law and liberty – improvements that were previously unimaginable. All people in rich societies today enjoy a higher living standard than Louis XIV – not a bad record for capitalism. But its history – measured against the 200,000 years of *Homo sapiens'* existence – is very short: a mere 200 years. And it is only in the last few decades that it has become a global phenomenon.

Most failed cultures have hung on for longer – eight hundred, nine hundred or a few thousand years – which further relativizes our sense of the sustainability of our own cultural model. Perhaps the fact that dead mass now exceeds living mass marks a tipping point – defined as the point beyond which something can no longer be corrected or restored to its previous state. Then again, perhaps there are no such points in human history given that our condition, as already mentioned, is already characterized by constant change and adaptation.

And by the ability to look ahead. What declining and defunct societies have lacked is the capacity to observe themselves from the outside, as in a thought experiment – just as I sometimes imagine historians 300 or 500 years hence might attempt to understand the at times curious world of the first quarter of the twenty-first century. Such an alienation effect would be illuminating, and useful when it comes to navigating our way out of blind alleys. In fact, modern societies ought to write their own obituaries setting out how, in retrospect, they would like to have seen themselves develop. Such an approach, from the standpoint of an imagined future, would free us from the tyranny of the present, in which too many decisions are taken based on our cultural subconscious. And it would free us from the boundless catastrophism in which we have become culturally entrenched owing to our fear that, whatever the future brings, it will inevitably be worse than the present. We must learn once again to see the future as a creative challenge, not as something we would rather avoid when so many things – global warming, biodiversity loss, the rise of dictators – loom darkly ahead.

But there is no end to history. History will only end when humankind has abolished itself. Or rather, *after* humankind has abolished itself. This is a meaningless sentence, for in that event, there will be no one around to register the fact. Any meaningful sentence presupposes the existence of a future world.[4] As long as we are still talking to each other, history has not come to an end.

The time before

It would, therefore, make little sense to write a book for the time after. What we need are books for the time *before*. Not another one on the fate of the world, climate disaster, species extinction, plastic pollution and impending doom. After all, these are books for the time after, when there will be no one left to read them.

Friends: let us rather concentrate on *the time before*! No more swan songs for the future. They are merely ritual invocations of the idea that there can be no end to history because such a thing must never be allowed to happen. All these invocations – it's not too late, there's still time, it's five minutes to midnight (how long have we been saying that?) – distract us perpetually from the simple fact that, before death, there is life. Therefore, we should – as individuals and as a society – organize our life in the meantime according to how we would one day like to be able to look back on it and ourselves.

I have seldom felt as melancholic as in the days following the death of Frank Schirrmacher, co-editor of the *Frankfurter*

Allgemeine Zeitung and head of its arts section. Few have received as many obituaries: so impressive and influential was his work that commentators were falling over themselves after his 'far too early' demise to list all the important and significant things he had said and done, and to bemoan this great loss to society.

And so on and so forth. What made me so sad was the fact that there was only one person who would never be able to read and appreciate all these tributes. That person was Frank Schirrmacher himself. As noted, any meaningful sentence must presuppose the existence of a future world. On that basis, obituaries would only be meaningful if they were written for the life before, not the life after – which, of course, does not exist.

Therefore, I say, everyone should write an obituary to themselves – in the sense of an account of how they would hope to have lived – while they are still alive. After death, that task falls to other people, by which time the content (by definition) no longer matters to the deceased, nor do they have any influence over it. I suspect that the task of writing your own obituary would be very productive, as it would oblige you to a certain extent to act like the person you would hope to have been. That would be much more constructive than just living from day to day and receiving an obituary at the end of it. If you're lucky, that is: after all, most people don't get one at all. You can read my own obituary on pp. 165–211 – but before that, let me tell you a few more stories.

The Great Refractor

One of the countless conferences on climate change and the necessary policy response took place at the site of the Great Refractor on Potsdam's Telegrafenberg. No idea exactly when: let's say ten years ago – it doesn't really matter. The Great

Refractor is what you might call the ultimate telescope: inau-
gurated in 1899 by Kaiser Wilhelm, it is a monument to the age
of science and technology, and remains the fourth largest in
the world. All very impressive.

I remember that conference not just because of the truly awe-
inspiring venue, but also because it was an 'open space' event,
meaning that there was – unusually – no fixed agenda, i.e.,
presentation, discussion, presentation, discussion and so on.
Instead, the participants could propose their own topics for the
sessions, whose results would then be presented and debated in
turn. A host of topics – carbon pricing, better communication of
climate issues, strategies for obtaining research funding – were
all readily adopted and discussed. For my part, I had proposed
the topic 'What if we fail?' It seemed logical to me to use this
'open space' forum to talk openly for once about the possibility
that, as things stood, all efforts to reach the 2° target postulated
at the time might fail and that, consequently, we would *not* be
able to halt the progress of climate change. What then?

Even today, at least a decade later, I still believe that our
ability to build a future for ourselves depends on being realistic
about the conditions for doing so, rather than simply cling-
ing to the hope that things will somehow turn out all right
in defiance of all data to the contrary. And in order to think
realistically, we have to factor in the possibility of failure, otherwise we won't know what measures and regulations need
to be devised in order to prevent failure or mitigate its consequences. Let's face it, we are much more likely to fail to limit
global warming to a 2° rise than we are to achieve it[5] – and
what then? Will that mean the end of the world? Or only the
end of climate politics? Will there no longer be any point in
modernizing human activity in such a way as to prevent, or at
least curb, the massive destruction of our vital resources? Or in
restoring ruined forests, waters, marshes and soils?

As such, the question 'What if we fail?' seemed to me a
very obvious one for a conference on climate change, quite

Fig. 1.2:   The Great Refractor: life is always better on the outside

apart from my own burning interest in the answer. Given its relevance to our survival, it is, after all, anything but trivial, especially if it remains unanswered. But there was only one other delegate besides me who was interested in the subject, so we chatted for a bit, missed everything else and had nothing substantial to contribute to the final plenary. By voting with their feet, the delegates had already given a sufficient empirical demonstration of their unwillingness to accord any relevance to the question of failure. 'What if we fail?' had been dropped from the agenda.

In the meantime, of course, the 2° target has been revised to 1.5°, regardless of the fact that emissions have since increased to such a level that the original 2° figure has become even less realistic than it already was. But such social realities are not allowed to get in the way of a scientific rationale which, based on highly complex measurements and calculations, insists on the necessity of such a limit.[6] If the science says 1.5°, then 1.5° it is. End of story. The trouble is, the climate pays no heed to such scientifically unassailable assertions but carries on warming away merrily as it deals with our ever-growing greenhouse gas output.

The fact that all this took place in a historic shrine to modern science struck me as highly symbolic. The vast room housing the Great Refractor was created exclusively for the purpose of looking out of it into the infinite expanse of the universe. Looking inwards, at ourselves and our own activity, was not part of the plan. Hence the name refractor, not reflector.

Ever since this episode, I have wondered why it is that scientific reason appears incapable of conceiving of the possibility that it could all go wrong. The simple truth is that that reason – a legacy of the Enlightenment – has no category of finitude and no strategy for stopping something it has once begun. Neither, as far as I can see, is there any scientific discipline focusing on the finite nature of human endeavours. While there are shelves upon shelves of apocalyptic writings – not just in the esoteric section but also under ecology and climatology – they all end not with the Lutheran sentiment 'let goods and kindred go, This mortal life also', but the predictable 'It's not too late.' Followed, equally predictably, by 'the comfortable small gestures of cycling, using energy-efficient bulbs, taking shorter showers and repairing electrical appliances', as Eva Horn, author of *The Future as Catastrophe*, observes with rightful exasperation.[7]

The concept of ending and finitude only occurs in non-scientific contexts – in lived experience, literature or art. And, of course, in religion, in the context of the Apocalypse. There is no place for it in the technical and scientific world, which is unhelpful when it comes to dealing with it as an actual problem. And that brings us back to the refractor: from there, we look outwards in the hope of discovering what exists outside the world. Outside the world there is the lure of infinity, the universe – a place without limits. And it is this notion of unlimited progress, of rolling back the boundaries of the possible, that constitutes the mythical basis of modern science; no one has ever been given a Nobel Prize for proving that something can't be done. Nobel Prizes are awarded to those who succeed in overcoming the limits of knowledge or perceived possibility. It is no coincidence that we date the beginning of modern science back to the decentring of our world view, when Copernicus displaced the Earth from the centre of the solar system and Galileo invented the telescope. Since we have ceased to be at the centre of things, we prefer to look outwards. And that's what the Great Refractor stands for: the infinite gaze.

Were we instead to look inwards, at ourselves and our own activity, our hopes and aspirations, there is one limit at least that we would be forced to address: the simple fact that, if anything is finite, it is, alas, our own lives. We all know that we are mortal, and it is an extremely uncomfortable fact. Death is incompatible with life because it is the opposite of life – and I will go on later to discuss why it is particularly incompatible with life in the modern era, and why it is perceived more than ever nowadays as so utterly out of place, frightening and antithetical to all our endeavours. But there it is: life is finite, and the grotesque idea of prolonging it infinitely by uploading the mind – or what we think of as the mind – to a hard disk speaks volumes about the fear of death experienced by those individuals who hope to defeat it through technology, if necessary by having themselves cryogenically frozen during their lifetime, to be thawed again once science has moved on a little.

Even before the first signs of a crisis of finitude start to appear in our cultural model, technical fantasies are already being mobilized: digitalization will bring about miraculous energy savings, hydrogen will save the day, electric cars will avert climate change and, ditto, green aircraft fuel. Instead of entertaining the possibility that less energy will be generated and consumed in future – for instance, because there are no more cars or planes – we celebrate tech heroes such as Elon Musk who have arrived on the scene two generations too late, courting and showering them with money even though they have nothing to offer beyond the mobility utopias of the fifties: rockets, cars and hyperloops – all things designed to take us somewhere at high speed, without ever stopping to ask ourselves what we plan to do when we get there. This future is an extremely outdated one, and merely tells the story of the loss of social and moral intelligence in the twenty-first century.

After all, civilization's greatest advances have been achieved through the improvement of inter-human relationships, and technology has only helped where people were able to use it to that end. The fact that there are far fewer victims of violence in modern societies than in medieval times is not due to better weapons technology or surveillance cameras but to the state monopoly on violence, and that is the result of social, not scientific, intelligence. Such intelligence must always be founded on a normative purpose, and what arises from it is not innovation but progress.

It is no accident that the concept of innovation seems to have replaced that of progress nowadays. Innovation needs no normative reference: to be innovative, a thing merely has to be newer than something else, regardless of whether that innovation was necessary. According to road safety statistics, more and more crashes are now caused by drivers being distracted from the road while scrolling through touchscreen sub-menus to adjust the windscreen wipers, for example. An old-fashioned lever on the steering wheel can be adjusted without looking: to transfer that function to an operating screen is innovative but idiotic. Progress, by contrast, is measured according to whether an innovation contributes something to a normatively justified end. If not, it can be dispensed with – just as developments that have become pointless or obsolete could be halted and dispensed with.

The trouble is we have no methodology for stopping because, in the magical thinking of our present symbolic universe, things go on for ever and problems of finitude are systemically non-existent. 'Away-from-here' is the only goal. Because we have no methodology for stopping, we never stop.

In the case of global warming, tackling this problem would mean stopping a lot of things, such as the mining of ever more raw materials in order to produce ever more products and services, for example. We would have to stop increasing the footprint of our economic metabolism and start reducing it. We would have to implement a methodology of finitude, and that means, quite simply, learning to stop. We would have to learn to recognize that life inevitably means death. As individuals, we cannot escape this lesson, however much we may resist it. As a society, we have a huge, highly developed and complex apparatus for avoiding it at all costs. In this respect, we are not a 'knowledge society' but a 'knowledge avoidance society'. As a culture, we have no concept of our own finiteness. Death is not a cultural category: in social terms, it simply doesn't exist.

Media in vita

By way of a brief interlude, here are two verses from the poem *Media in vita* (1931) by Theobald Tiger (a pseudonym of the German-Jewish satirist Kurt Tucholsky):

Every morning when I'm shaving in the lamplight's glow,
I soap my face and think: just x times minus one to go.
And there I stand in foamy piety
Brooding on my own mortality.
There where the parallels intersect, that's where I too
    must fly,
Ah, how I will miss myself when in my grave I lie.
And others too –? If they have eyes to see they'll take the
    view
That dying is like pulling out a spoon that's stuck in glue.

Dead people have no problems

'Death is a problem of the living. Dead people have no problems.' With this laconic remark, the sociologist Norbert
Elias shows himself to be very much part of an enlightened,
post-metaphysical culture in which a dead person is regarded
unequivocally as a lifeless body; as matter without consciousness, it can have no feelings and hence no problems. On a
rational level – that is, within the context of our modern
reason – we will concur with this view, but whether we do so
on an emotional level is far less certain. Chances are we will
still catch ourselves occasionally – at funerals or when passing
through a cemetery – pondering the uncomfortable question
of what it must be like to be dead. And that question is only
uncomfortable because, when we try to imagine it, we still
think of ourselves as having some kind of self-consciousness.
Consequently, questions that seem on the face of it to be
straightforward – such as organ donation, burial or cremation,
wills, living wills and the like – turn out, when applied to ourselves, to be much less clear. After all, when we reflect on such
things, we are picturing ourselves in a state that we cannot
know while we are alive. Between you and me, whenever I'm
in a cemetery, I can't help thinking it must be unpleasant to

be buried next to someone you can't stand. Or too close to the road. It's strange when you think about it: we all know for certain that we will die, but no one knows what it's like to be dead.

It is precisely for this reason that scholars who have studied man's relationship with death, whether from a philosophical, sociological or physiological perspective, have found it so fascinating. For humans are – or so we assume – the only animals that are aware of their mortality, yet they are no less helpless in the face of it than any other species. When we think about the end of life, we inevitably get into another philosophical category which, once again, is something that presumably only humans agonize over, namely the meaning of life. Even if you consider life and the universe to be essentially meaningless, and can think of no better answer to the 'meaning of life, the universe and everything' than Douglas Adams's supercomputer which, after several million years, finally spits out the number 42, you would still find it unsatisfying to sum up your own precious life, its hopes, disappointments, successes and failures, triumphs and embarrassments in this way. Our own life is far from being a matter of indifference to us. At least, in most cases.

No doubt about it: death – what Ernst Bloch calls 'the great In-Vain' – stands coolly and matter-of-factly in the way of all our desires for permanence, eternity and immortality, and that modern fantasy of uploading the contents of our minds to a hard disk in the hope of some kind of post-mortal mental life is no more realistic than the hope of being reborn as another being, transitioning to a new form of existence as a light, spirit or astral being, going to heaven or hell, or – if you died a good martyr – having sex with seventy-two virgins. Whatever the prospects, they are by no means assured, and even an Islamic State fighter is terrified of being killed by a Kurdish Peshmerga and losing his prime spot in macho martyrs' heaven. The afterworld is an uncertain place.

That nagging uncertainty over death and the presumable eternity awaiting us beyond it is of course particularly

prevalent in our secularized modern world, where the main
reason that death has no proper place is that neither heaven
nor hell, nor any kind of afterworld, can be located empirically;
consequently, it has to be assigned to a compartment which
lies outside our rational comfort zone, and into which we are
loath to venture unless we have to. In other words, death is
cognitively alien to the modern age, whose whole self-identity
rests on the notion that all natural processes can be explained
– if not immediately, then at least a step at a time – by an ever-
evolving science. But even though we may be able to decode
the genome, photograph black holes and visualize brain activity with imaging techniques, use artificial intelligence to help
detect tumours and develop vaccines in hitherto unimaginable
time frames, the fact remains that no one knows what death is.
Let alone how to abolish it. On that front, all science is helpless. In other words, Death is the opposite of Enlightenment,
the final mystery, an uncomfortable reminder that knowledge
has its limits and, alas, that every life is finite.

I have just read a couple of works on 'the history of death'
and 'death, modernity and society' because it troubles me that
our modern society has *no* relationship with death and hence
with finitude, and that this curious fact has a lot to do with the
inability to stop which has increasingly shaped our cultural
model since the rise of growth-based capitalism. And if we're
not able to stop, then we'll never be able to deal with the problems of finitude, such as climate change or species extinction.
It's as simple as that.

By contrast, it is undoubtedly the case that premodern societies *did* have a connection with death – indeed, they had to,
for many different reasons. In times when life expectancy was
less than thirty years (as it was around 1700), or less than forty
years (as was still the case in Germany until a mere 150 years
ago), death was always close at hand, or at least closer than
today, when we are statistically likely to live twice as long.
Average life expectancy has grown in tandem with the rise

of industrial capitalism and hence of modern western-style society; in the case of Germany, to quote the market research company Statista, 'between 1871/1881 and 1949/1951 alone, average life expectancy at birth rose by 29 years for men and 30 years for women. In the second half of the twentieth and the early part of the twenty-first century, between 1949/1951 and 2016/18, average life expectancy at birth rose by 13.9 years for men and 14.8 years for women.'[8]

Such an extension of our lifespan would have been unthinkable at the beginning of the nineteenth century, and it is not the result of medical progress alone, though this is often claimed. True, we can now cure many diseases that people were still dying from only a few decades ago, but even the great victories in the fight against infectious diseases can be distorted by statistical effects. After all, some individuals have always managed to reach a ripe old age – but only a few. Most perished in younger years, from causes such as inflamed tooth roots, appendicitis or cholera, but also – and here's the point – a general level of violence that made the chances of dying an 'unnatural' death much higher than in modern constitutional states.[9]

In short, it is not the march of science alone that has prolonged the life of large numbers of people: advances in the organization of human coexistence – what we call the civilizing process – are also responsible for increasing the interval between birth and death to such an extraordinary extent.

At a psychological level, however, this means that, since death no longer looms on the horizon from early adulthood but is normally associated with 'old age', we don't need to give it any serious thought for five or six decades. For the greater part of our life, death isn't that important.

Another statistical factor affecting average life expectancy is infant and child mortality. Around 1820, a fifth of all children died at birth, and a further third failed to reach adulthood. In such circumstances, the death of a child was a routine occurrence – not that that made it any less painful for the parents, of course. After the death of his eight-year-old son Edgar, Karl Marx writes in a letter of 1855 to Friedrich Engels, for example: 'It is impossible to describe how much we miss him all the time. I have suffered all sorts of misfortune, but now I know what real misfortune is.'[10]

Today, when infant mortality in a country like Germany is below 0.4%, and 99% of a birth cohort reach adulthood, the death of a child is a shocking exception, yet well into the nineteenth century it was – however sad for those affected – an everyday reality. And the same thing applies throughout the human lifecycle: under the medical, hygiene and legal conditions of medieval times, life security as a whole was extremely low compared with today, and death therefore much more present in everyday life. (The importance of the rule of law, food security and protection from violence can be seen to this this day in so-called failed states where – as in Nigeria, for example – life expectancy is around thirty years lower than in Germany.)

In premodern societies, death belonged to the category of events that could happen at any time, whether to oneself or to others. As such, it would surely have been emotionally unsustainable to invest in our attitude to it the degree of fear and dread inspired in us today by the mere thought of our demise, let alone the experience of losing someone close, especially when it comes 'far too early'. There is a limit to the amount of misfortune we can cope with; where death is omnipresent, our emotional response to it has to be scaled down somewhat.

In his theory of civilization, Norbert Elias has shown that changes in social conditions and inter-human relationships always go hand in hand with changes in our psychology – sociogenesis and psychogenesis are, in his words, two sides of the same coin. Thus the response to loss, the experience of violence and coercion, and the emotions of affection and love are just as much subject to historical evolution as the relationship

to the self. Elias has demonstrated this in detail with reference
to the development of table manners and norms of politeness
in relation to changing levels of violence, and we can appreciate the connection between psycho- and sociogenesis simply
by considering how our tolerance of unpleasant odours (or
those perceived as such) has lessened by comparison with the
days when there were no sewage systems and people rarely
washed. Or how sick the first railway passengers became from
the dizzying new speed of travel.

In his studies, Elias shows in particular how longer chains
of interdependence, involving the cooperation and mutual
reliance of more and more people, produce whole new patterns of perception and emotion. The ability to take the 'long
view' is one example: here, the immediate impulses of hatred,
revenge and retaliation are deferred and gradually replaced by
behaviours of social distance and politeness, as the evolution of
table manners shows. Elias's perhaps most important insight
is that coercion and violence change over the course of the
civilizing process so that people learn, without the external
threat of force, to conform to norms and laws, cultivate virtues
such as punctuality and courtesy, educate themselves and so
on. Eventually, external restraint becomes self-restraint, and
the more people's behaviour is regulated and choreographed
by such internal restraints, the less violent their coexistence
becomes. While such psychological and sociological consequences of the civilizing process should not be thought of as
irreversible (Elias himself talks about de-civilizing processes
such as Nazism, for example), from a long-term perspective
the effects of civilization are generally a significant fall in the
level of violence and greater self-restraint on the part of the
individual.

As a further consequence, emotional outbursts of overwhelming hatred or unbridled joy also become fewer, our
emotional state becomes more muted, and much of what was
formerly vented (in medieval times, for instance) in the form

of direct aggression towards others is now turned inwards –
something that can cause major problems for the individual, as
demonstrated by the well-developed and flourishing therapy
industry. Even the processes of the brain have changed in the
modern age, right down to the level of neuronal organization
(see p. 102).

All this simply goes to show that expectations of normality
are extremely variable – as we have currently seen for ourselves with the COVID pandemic – and so are behavioural
norms and their emotional corollaries: what was pronounced
the 'new normal' in 2021 –wearing masks, social distancing,
regular sanitizing, staying at home, etc., etc. – would have been
regarded as totally abnormal in 2019. And however temporary
this episode may prove to be, a great many people will have
experienced marked changes in their emotional state. So how
much more, then, do long-term changes in social relationships,
in codes of etiquette and interdependencies, and in behavioural
standards and expectations influence psychological structures,
including our attitude to death?

Tamed death

Philippe Ariès's monumental work *The Hour of Our Death*
attempts to provide substantive answers to this question.
In it, he charts the key stages of the evolution in social attitudes to death as reflected in the development of cemeteries,
headstones, mourning rituals and wills (particularly from the
French historical perspective). The most obvious difference by
comparison with today is what Ariès calls 'the public quality
of death'.

In the premodern age, death was not only, as discussed,
an omnipresent phenomenon: it was also public in the sense
that there were often many people present at both deathbed
and wake – from family members, the priest and sometimes

a doctor, to friends and neighbours. According to Ariès, this public treatment of death persisted into the late nineteenth century – so much so, in fact, that it drew complaints from doctors and hygienists, albeit to little avail. The reason for this was the sheer pervasiveness of death in people's lives: the numbers of deceased alone would have made the complex endeavour of relegating death and dying to a behind-the-scenes role inconceivable. So public was the whole business that, when a priest was called to a dying person, strangers in the street could accompany him all the way to the house and bedside. There were even 'wailing women' who performed the rituals of mourning and lamentation despite having no personal connection with the deceased – a further illustration of the routineness of death.[11] Three or four generations ago, the idea that someone should face death alone in a hospital or nursing-home room would have seemed just as bizarre as the presence of a complete stranger at the deathbed of a deceased family member does to us today.

In my own case, after receiving news of my father's death in the early hours of the morning, I was astonished, on arriving two or three hours later, to find a group of neighbours gathered in the house. I can still clearly remember how unusual, but also how extremely helpful, I found it to be part of a group of mourners, even though I only knew most of those present from a distance. Here, too, death was still to some extent a public matter in the sense that Ariès describes. That said, this was in a rural community in the 1990s, and my father hadn't died in hospital: it is, after all, important to allow for local differences in customs and traditions before making historical generalizations. Based on my personal experience, however, I would certainly say that the public nature of death made the situation easier for the living than if it had been a purely private affair, or indeed taken place in an institutional setting.

Another significant – and in my view the most important – difference between past and present attitudes to death is the belief in the continuation of life after the death of the body. Of course, people have always known that the rotting and decaying body of a dead person is no longer (except for a brief transitional phase) alive, but there was always – depending on the prevailing vision of the afterlife – the prospect of the soul or the spirit or some other spiritual essence living on after the biological end of bodily existence. And this is duly reflected in codes of conduct around the body and in preservation and burial rituals, which show great historical and cultural variation. Corpses were cremated, buried with other family members, children or pets, equipped with various objects for the journey to the afterlife, boiled in order to strip the flesh from the enduring skeleton, or buried in the ground, in caves, houses, crypts, under trees, in churches and so on. Essentially, there are only two common threads here: first, an awareness of death and mortality is evident right from the earliest proven burials (dating back over 100,000 years – even the Neanderthals buried their dead), making it one of the few anthropological constants.

Second, the idea that there is *nothing* after death is a distinctly modern one – the millennia preceding the Enlightenment generally offered the happy advantage that the life of the individual appeared embedded in a cosmology which did not regard the end of earthly life as the end of life per se, and which, depending on the prevailing religious superstructure and the wretchedness of people's earthly existence, could make the hereafter appear far more attractive than life on earth.

And however much these notions vary, just as the process of dying itself varies from a gradual passage through transitional states into the realm of the dead to the medical pronouncement of brain death according to defined criteria, Ariès is surely right to conclude that 'Until the age of scientific progress, human beings accepted the idea of a continued existence after death.'[12] Up to then, this belief was part of an overarching symbolic universe that had embedded individual destiny

Fig. 1.3: A Neanderthal pondering the existence of nothingness

within a God-given order and ensured the 'integration of death within the paramount reality of social existence'.[13]

The term 'symbolic universe' is used by the sociologists Peter Berger and Thomas Luckmann to mean a frame of reference within which the members of a society can categorize the conditions of their existence and the explanations of various phenomena – that is, it allows the individual to understand the meaning of their essence and existence within an unquestioned order and to live accordingly. The modern age offers a symbolic universe characterized by categories such as causality, cause and effect, laws of nature, predictability, order, logic and so on, and in which nothing exists that cannot be scientifically proven. In this symbolic universe, the unexplained is simply regarded as the not-yet-explained. Such a universe has no place for a hereafter: it is an eternal here and now. By contrast, the symbolic universes of premodern epochs had the capacity to offer an overarching interpretive system, such as a divine will and decree that is expressed in the death of a human being. Religions offer a way of ordering one's own existence within a meaningful whole so that unsettling questions about the meaning of life never arise. The symbolic universe of the modern age, by contrast, is characterized not by the uniformity but by the differentiation of its interpretative approach. This is why everything always seems so complicated – even things that are actually quite simple. In his essay *Anthropology from a Pragmatic Point of View*, Kant already refers to the resulting phenomenon of hyperrationality and the tendency to 'rave with reason' (ironically, this is the very essay which, in these times of anti-colonial and anti-racist hyperrationality, has brought the Enlightenment thinker into disrepute as racist and sexist – a neat illustration of where differentiation can lead).

In a premodern world, 'the symbolic universe shelters the individual from ultimate terror by bestowing ultimate legitimation upon the protective structures of the institutional order.'[14] And the existence of that order is made palpably real by the dominant institutions of the church and nobility.

The symbolic universe is also experienced on a practical level in the sense that the prevailing order cannot be dissolved or overcome by the individual – the daughter of a serf cannot emancipate herself from her lot and become something other than what was preordained for her at birth by going to college and getting a degree. In such a premodern order, there are no individual avenues of opportunity and no careers in the modern sense. The permanence of the status quo is also constantly reinforced by the complete absence of any scope for forging one's own path, or shaping one's own life story in the modern sense.

Even so, within such an order, which undergoes a radical transformation with the Enlightenment, industrialization, the rise of science and the emergence of bourgeois society, death and dying can be categorized as part of the essence of the world. For this reason, Ariès calls premodern death 'tamed death'. The death we know today he calls 'wild death' because it is perceived by the individual as an aggressive superior force they are powerless to conquer.

The yawning gulf

It is not until secularization, and with it the release of human existence from the heteronomy of church dogma and similarly inclined secular orders, that people are suddenly able to die their own, personal death. Although the question of the accountability and godliness of the individual way of life emerges as early as the sixth century with the Rule of Saint Benedict, it is still a good millennium before we begin to see the individualization of human life and the development of notions of autonomy over individual existence, and hence of the assumption of responsibility for one's own life. Thereafter, the rationalism of the Enlightenment gradually establishes the image of man as an adult being capable of autonomous judgement and responsible for himself and the community as a whole, and with the capacity, through education and upbringing, to reach a point where he can apply his reason in the interests of a better world order. In so doing, he acts freely and to the best of his knowledge and belief, ideally with no obligation except to the categorical imperative, as formulated by Kant: 'Act only according to that maxim whereby you can, at the same time, will that it should become a universal law.'

The development of human societies is characterized by sudden surges of individualization during which people's self-image and their relationships to and with each other change. These surges depend on cultural developments: thus a highly differentiated society based on the division of labour needs people who want to 'make something of themselves', whereas a medieval feudal society with no social mobility emphatically does not. When the Enlightenment, in particular, became the dominant paradigm – indeed the framework of the modern symbolic universe – it ushered in an individualization process that is still ongoing. Being an individual by no means implies an easier life, as it comes with greater pressure to forge one's own path and exercise freedom and self-responsibility. Such demands are synonymous with modernity, and many of us feel the urge to flee them from time to time by letting off steam at the football stadium, partying to excess or indulging in intoxicants of various kinds. *Escape from Freedom* is the title of a book by Erich Fromm who – like Hannah Arendt, for example – saw that, as well as releasing us from the burden of constraint, freedom also saddles us with the burden of decision making. And with the advent of individualization in the modern age, people had to begin not only to live their own life, but also to die their 'own death'.

That death no longer took the form of a routinely expected public occurrence but became an increasingly private matter – not so much part of an all-encompassing and intact symbolic universe but more of an individual experience. Consequently, the question of the meaning of life and the necessity of confronting one's own mortality had to be handled without any form of collective embedding to alleviate the depressing prospect of one's own annihilation. 'Throughout the seventeenth and eighteenth centuries,' Ariès summarizes with poetic emphasis, 'there is a kind of inexorable downward movement on all levels of society towards the yawning gulf of nothingness.'[15]

While this may be laying it on a bit thick, people today do have to take far more responsibility for themselves and for their present and future identity, without the possibility of recourse to an all-powerful fate or divine will. And if we set this alongside the diminishing importance of the institution traditionally responsible for the interpretation and ritualization of birth, death and other life events – the Church – we can see that modern human beings are, comparatively speaking, much more alone when it comes to giving meaning to their life, and particularly their death. Berger and Luckmann, and also recently Peter Sloterdijk,[16] have pointed out that, with the loss of the integrative function of religious interpretive approaches, the Church has also seen a radical change in its social function: it is no longer the representative and agent of a universally valid and unquestioned order, and its role in terms of the division of social responsibilities is now reduced to the ritualization of milestones such as birth, confirmation or communion, marriage and death. The more such milestones have escaped the bounds of the premodern order and symbolic universe, the more private they have become as events that can be celebrated or not – there is no obligation to do so. In pluralized settings, the Church serves first and foremost as a guide to life situations for which private or state institutions have nothing to offer. It retains its monopoly on ritual, but is no longer an ordering force.

Philosophy has no answers either

All this has come about not as a sudden revolution but as a process of change occurring unevenly over centuries, and responsibilities for interpreting such changes have shifted accordingly. With the disappearance of the religiously endorsed and ecclesiastically orchestrated belief that death was a fate that was part of the symbolic universe and that life would continue after death, the problem of death increasingly became a matter for philosophy. Put simply, it wasn't until the Enlightenment that death became a problem at all in this sense – that is, for the individual – and one that needed solving through diverse intellectual efforts.

For anyone interested in the philosophical history of this development, I recommend the excellent overview by Armin Nassehi and Georg Weber.[17] For my part, I am in no position to do justice to the various philosophical exercises on the nature and meaning of death, from Heidegger's 'being-towards-death'

through Ernst Bloch's 'red hero' who, 'enshrined in the heart of the working class', overcomes the disadvantages of his individual death to survive in the collective consciousness, to Sartre, for whom everything dissolves into absurdity: '. . . it is meaningless that we are born, it is meaningless that we die.'

Well, hallelujah! As far as I can see, despite all these philosophical endeavours, death has remained an unsolved problem in the modern age, and one that resists all explanation because it lies outside the realm of thought and conceivability. There is a philosophical current that has always emphasized this fact. It ranges from Epicurus ('Death does not concern us, because as long as we exist, death is not here. And once it does come, we no longer exist. Therefore it concerns neither the living nor the dead') through Ludwig Wittgenstein ('The solution to the riddle of life in space and time lies outside space and time') to Groucho Marx ('Why should I care about posterity? What's posterity ever done for me?'), and is to my mind the most epistemologically appealing.

The very attempt to explain death in the mode of enlightened thinking illustrates the perhaps irreconcilable tension between the fact that humans are animals and, as such, subject to the laws of biology, and the fact that they have developed a co-evolutionary mode of life and survival which emancipates them from nature. Death marks the precise point at which man as a natural being must – despite all his technological inventions for controlling the living world and all his culture – yield to nature. As a biological fact, death is acultural: it is one hundred per cent nature. Where life ends, so does co-evolution. A dead body has a biochemistry but no culture – a fact which enlightenment fails to acknowledge.

No one has articulated this absolute limit of enlightenment more clearly than Max Horkheimer and Theodor W. Adorno in their *Dialectic of Enlightenment*: 'Any attempt to break the compulsion of nature by breaking nature only succumbs more deeply to that compulsion.'[18] This is the point beyond which enlightenment cannot go. And at which the individual fantasy of immortality coincides with a cultural fantasy of overcoming finitude.

In short, philosophy is no better at solving the intractable problem that, sadly, we must all experience death for ourselves, yet we know neither what it will be like nor what comes next. This is what is so scary about death, and the less you are able to believe in God and heaven and hell, the more frightening and perplexing it becomes. In other words, what was less troublesome for people for a couple of thousand years because they were able to believe in something that lay 'outside space and time' only really became a problem in the secularized modern age, and one that could only be solved via one of two strategies: first, by making death invisible, and second – as already touched on – by privatizing it.

As we saw, increased life expectancy and the slowing of the ageing process thanks to spectacular medical and scientific advances have helped subordinate the fact of death to the demands of the here and now – death will come at some point, but there are more important things to worry about in the meantime. Furthermore, apart from state funerals or death notices, deaths are an entirely private matter – if you have never had anything to do with the person in question, their death is not an event that commands attention. In normal circumstances, just over 900,000 people die every year in Germany – an average of nearly 2,500 every day – but, except in the case of pandemics or disasters such as plane crashes, no one takes any notice. Even hearses have disappeared; you read the odd death notice in the paper and that's it. One of the reasons for this is that four-fifths of all deaths occur in hospitals or nursing homes, where the person's demise and the care of their body are in professional hands and thus remain as hidden from the outside world as conceivably possible.

This remoteness and invisibility of the private death also leads to a curious uncertainty in our approach to dying or seriously ill people. It is as if the absence of death in every-day life has left us with no script for speaking about death: should we mention it when talking to someone who is fatally ill? Should we avoid the subject at all costs because neither the afflicted person nor we ourselves know what to say? I had this very same experience in my last conversation with a terminally ill friend who talked euphorically about taking up a guest professorship in Canada the following spring, and how I absolutely must come with him: we would do great things. A week later he was dead, and I can't say that we ever found a way of addressing his impending death. In fact we deliberately ignored it in a kind of mutual deception, perhaps from a need to protect each other. Two full-grown men, intellectual, dynamic and sharp as you like, yet utterly unable to find the right words.

Or to put it another way, the invisibility of death robbed us of the ability to find the right emotion for dealing with it as an unavoidable fact. Dying and death are, as Norbert Elias put it, 'a blank area on the social map'.[19] Even if things have changed considerably since the time when Elias wrote his reflections on the 'loneliness of the dying', and we are able to look back today on the development of an elaborate system of palliative medicine, with the establishment of hospices marking a major advance compared with those days, it is undeniable that death and the treatment of the dying have not become generalized as a fact of everyday life but rather professionalized: in addition to medical and care staff and chaplaincy services, there are now also therapists and end-of-life support providers on the scene. And even euthanasia doctors. On 26 February 2020, the German Constitutional Court recognized the right to a self-determined death, thereby opening the door to profes-sional-assisted suicide, which was illegal in Germany up to that point. With this judgment, the highest authority in the land decreed that 'a person has sovereignty not just over their life, but also, and in all respects, over their death.' Thus writes the legal philosopher Uwe Volkmann, adding 'In this way, that death is also fully secularized; there is no longer anything transcendental about it, as if it were a bridge to another world. Death is an object of human disposal, a matter of individual determination, the implementation of which can even – as in the case of commercial assisted-dying organizations – be turned into a recognized profession.'[20] This is what we call the functional differentiation of modern societies: with new problems comes the creation of new institutions and new professions. Or, if you like, positions of responsibility designed to help ensure that, while death is in good hands, it can (for that very reason) still remain outside the realm of everyday life, invisible in normal circumstances. Death is a private matter.

Funerals are restricted, as often stated in death notices, to 'close family members', and here too there are specialists – from the priest to the celebrant to the undertakers – who are responsible for the professional side of things. And the more death has shifted, in the wake of individualism, from a public to a personal matter, the more private most people's approach to it has become. *Ars moriendi* – the art of dying – is as much a thing of the past as the multi-functionality of cemeteries, which have at times been used not just for burying the dead but also as places of sanctuary, and have, moreover, varied in form and location throughout history. The typical quiet, secluded grounds and chapel that we know today are, historically speaking, a relatively new phenomenon, which Ariès attributes to a gradual trend between the fifteenth and nineteenth centuries towards extending the act of memorialization to more and more people, while at the same time building cemeteries further away from churches and hence the centre of town. Death was to be kept literally separate from life.

It was, incidentally, this very invisibility and privacy of death that made the images of stacked coffins in Bergamo and mass graves and refrigerated trucks in New York appear so shocking in the early days of the pandemic: the idea that people were dying in their droves, and to such an extent that the existing

Fig. 1.4:   In the midst of life: mass graves in New York, 2020

death management facilities were overloaded and forced to improvise, was simply not part of our death-denying symbolic universe.

This was the truly unsettling thing about the COVID pandemic: it brought the everyday, ongoing and unstoppable phenomenon of death back into the world of the living, where it has had no place in modern societies. For this reason, it is unsurprising that there is no remembrance culture around the millions of COVID deaths. For individual deaths of famous personalities such as Princess Diana, there are now standardized rituals: we lay flowers, light candles and tweet our condolences. For disasters such as plane crashes, the procedure is the same as for school shootings or terror attacks: we mourn from a distance, and presidents utter stock phrases.

But in all these cases, death and the dead are abnormalities, radical exceptions that have nothing to do with our familiar world. There is no social role for death in the modern age. It is by definition an individual matter, the end of a private life, impacting only on individual family members, friends and loved ones. And isn't it utterly astonishing that schools and businesses remained open during the COVID crisis long after visits to the dying and funerals for larger groups had been prohibited? Nothing could bring home the privatization of death more strongly than the fact that, during the pandemic, the business of dying and death was consigned to those private contacts regarded as avoidable. At the same time, people were allowed to attend league football matches, work on meat-factory assembly lines or shop at DIY stores.

And inherent in the atmosphere of silence that surrounds every private death is an aesthetic that treats it as something it's best not to talk about, something to be dealt with ourselves in 'silent contemplation', something that is strangely absent from the communicative landscape of everyday life and normality. The American title of a Hans Fallada novel says it all: *Every Man Dies Alone.* So alone, in fact, that we can hardly imagine our own death as anything other than a private matter, and prefer not to talk or think about it because of the oppressive anxiety it arouses. At the same time, however, we can't shut out our awareness of death, and we therefore seek to gain a psychological advantage by training ourselves to act as if we were in fact immortal. We can then apply this practice socially – even culturally – *as a solution to the fundamental aporia of Enlightenment*, and act collectively as if there were no end, no boundary, no limitations. Which is where we are currently at as a society.

That is, unless we happen to die in the meantime. As I found out on 22 April 2020.

Heart attack

The 22nd of April, 2020 was a Wednesday. Two days before, on the Monday morning, I had already had a funny feeling while cycling, as if I was being pulled back on a rubber band

as I tried to pedal forwards. This was followed in the night
by a slight shortness of breath, but I just put it down to an
allergy, a reaction to the pollen – it was spring, after all. The
next day I was on the phone for a long time while out walking,
and it happened again: an oppressive feeling – unspecific, but
uncomfortable. It went away after half an hour.

Right, I think, better arrange another check-up with the
internist to be on the safe side. I manage to get an appointment
for Thursday: perfect. Probably nothing to worry about. For
some reason, angina springs to mind. I google, and although
most of the symptoms don't apply, I learn that angina is not the
disease itself but merely a symptom of coronary heart disease.
OK, but was what I just had angina?

Wednesday. In the morning, I do a Zoom recording for
Swiss TV – a philosophical discussion programme presented
by the wonderful Barbara Bleisch. Since it's become the norm
nowadays (we are in the first COVID wave) to slouch in front
of your home-office camera in your scruffy old clothes, I decide
to be different and put on a suit, shirt and tie (which I never
wear normally). The recording goes without a hitch. Then I
make myself a coffee, get changed and sit out on the balcony.
Another bout of breathlessness, this time very unpleasant and
coupled with a distinct feeling of anxiety. I google again, only
mildly concerned at this stage: where is the nearest cardiologist? OK, a fair way, but it's still afternoon and the practice is
open, according to the internet.

My part of town is no good for cycling: rough cobblestones
everywhere. So I set off on foot. It's about half an hour to the
Cardiology Centre. My anxiety grows. About halfway, a police
car comes towards me and I wonder whether I should stop it,
but decide not to. Don't be ridiculous, it's probably nothing. I
keep going in a state of rising anxiety. When I finally get there,
I get the wrong house number and can't find the Cardiology
Centre. During the search, I bump into Phil, a familiar face. He
wants to talk. I say – I don't know why – 'Phil, I can't stop, I'm

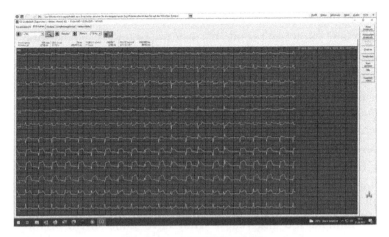

Fig. 1.5:   My ECG: OMG!

about to kick the bucket.' And I finally find the entrance to the
practice. First floor: I ring the bell. 'I'd like to see the doctor',
I say and am handed the usual forms to fill in. My hands are
shaking slightly: it'll be a job to read my writing. But the doctor
calls me into her surgery before I've even finished. I sit down
in the visitor's chair, at a COVID-compliant distance from her
desk. I've hardly begun to describe my symptoms when she
interrupts me: 'We won't waste any time on your medical history, let's do an ECG straightaway. Come with me, please.' At
reception, she gives the nurse instructions, and I follow her
into another room and lie on the couch while the nurse hooks
me up to the ECG. A few minutes later, the doctor comes in,
looks at the screen and says 'Oh, my God!'

It's never a good sign when a doctor says 'Oh, my God',
I think to myself as I lie there. She looks at me – these are
COVID times and we are all wearing masks, so you don't see
much of people's faces – and says: 'I'm afraid you're having
a heart attack.' My mind goes numb. *Me? I'm* having a heart
attack? Why? I can't be. How come? I just walked in here
right as rain. The doctor registers my incomprehension. 'Yes,
I'm afraid you're having an acute heart attack. We'll ring the

emergency doctor now, and you'll be taken straightaway to the cath lab.' I still can't think, it's as if my brain's been anaesthetized. The doctor disappears (to fetch a defibrillator, as I later learn), comes back, injects me with something. She probably explains it all, but none of it makes sense. When I eventually manage, through a small chink in my sudden debility, to ask what happens next, she says: 'I told you, the emergency doctor is on his way; they'll take you to the cath lab, and they'll take it from there.' It's all Greek to me, I probably ask more questions, what does that mean, but to be honest I've forgotten all the details. A few minutes later, two paramedics arrive, in the familiar red and yellow. They have some sort of folding contraption with them. They stand around; we wait for the emergency doctor. I lie on the couch, mental capacity zero. Eventually ask if I can put my shirt back on. Yes. I feel I'm surrounded by professionals who know what to expect; I'm the only one in the dark here. Heart attack. I'm having a heart attack. I must be going into hospital now, otherwise the paramedics wouldn't be here. Oh, my God. No one does anything for the time being; we wait.

The emergency doctor comes, speaks to the cardiologist, it's about which hospital to go to, I think they ask me about it, I have no opinion (I don't know any hospitals), the paramedics unfold their trolley, I am lifted off the couch – why can't I walk? What happens now? The paramedics wheel me to the exit, the doctor is standing there; she has tears in her eyes! Even through her glasses and mask, she looks quite despairing. I look at her. She says: 'I'm really crossing my fingers for you!' Twice she says it. With tears in her eyes. I think: Shit! You're a goner, old man.

The paramedics wheel me to the lift and we go down. Surreal: where I came in on my own two feet half an hour ago I'm now being wheeled out on a trolley. It's broad daylight, people are doing their shopping, all is business as usual; ahead is the ambulance with the flashing blue light. I am wheeled inside; the doctor gets in with me and makes a phone call. The ambulance moves off, nee-naw, nee-naw. From where I'm lying, I can only see out of the clear bit above the blacked-out windows: house fronts, sky, treetops. I lie there while the ambulance turns left, left again, right. Eventually, we're on the motorway. So this is dying? I think, in a strangely matter-of-fact way. Is this what it feels like? I ask the doctor if I can use the phone. I call my wife, shock at the other end: which hospital? I ask the doctor (I know nothing): Westend Hospital? Westend Hospital. 'I don't know anything, heart attack, I'll ring again.' Will I ring again? I phone my son, same conversation. Big shock again. Of course. And I still feel so weirdly detached, keep thinking the same thing: is this what dying is like?

It's a long drive in the ambulance. Eventually, we seem to turn off the motorway; the vehicle stops, it's eerily quiet. From the front, I hear: 'Shit, the siren's not working!' Someone gets out, runs past the window, calls: 'You go ahead, our siren's on the blink.' Funny, there must be two ambulances, I hadn't realized. At last, nee-naw, nee-naw again, then we turn into a compound with that familiar hospital look, I can see brick facades out of the top of the windows, old-style architecture. The ambulance stops, I hear an exchange: 'No, not here, you want to go down there . . .' Doors slam, the ambulance starts up again, swings round fast. Then it stops a second time; this time the rear doors are opened, the paramedics wheel me out on the trolley, up to the main entrance. There are three or four people there in the green scrubs you see in films. One of them looks at me and says 'Hiya!' I say 'Hiya!' back. Well, that's something, at least: you wouldn't say 'Hiya' to a corpse.

I am transferred to another trolley and wheeled to a huge room, where I am lifted from trolley two onto a table. The green team do an incredible number of things simultaneously, or so it seems to me. I am fitted with tubes, attached to various drips. I am told a catheter will be passed through my artery to my heart from my wrist or, failing that, from my groin.

OK. I am covered with a sheet (did I get undressed?), answer questions (I can't remember a single one), then the catheterization process begins. Amazing: you can see the tube being guided towards your own heart on the screen. I don't know if I want to see it or not. The catheterization surgeon – it says 'Dr Wensel' on his badge – does his stuff with an extraordinary air of calm and confidence; indeed, there is something hugely reassuring about the professionalism of everything from the 'Hiya' onwards. No one is agitated, everyone seems to know what they're doing and what they have to do. I am fitted with a stent. One of my coronary arteries was completely blocked, hence the heart attack. The members of the team seem satisfied. Then I am taken to the intensive care unit. So they tell me. Fair enough. By this stage, I'm no longer thinking, not because my brain has packed up, but because my status is now that of a patient. They will know what to do with me.

An Eastern European male nurse arrives with a bed onto which I am transhipped. Corridors, lifts, underground passageways, lifts, between them a whole series of doors: this is a long journey. At one turn – I can't believe my eyes – stands my wife. She can only look. It's COVID time, no visits are allowed, especially between theatre and intensive care. I probably tell her everything's OK. Wave bye bye. The nurse keeps on pushing, corridors, doors, doors, corridors, lift. Then intensive care, my final destination – for now. It must be about half three or four in the afternoon by this time. A couple of hours ago, I was sitting at my desk doing a TV interview.[21] (Dr Opitz, the senior consultant, explained to me a few days later that 40 per cent of those with the same diagnosis as me don't survive. Gulp. At the Westend Hospital, I was 'the guy who walks for half an hour to the doctor's with an acute heart attack'.)

Now, though, I am lying in the ICU, dazed, uncomprehending, my brain still very sluggish. There's an old girl next to me on my right – as I, with my intimacy phobia, am quick to register. No chance of privacy here. You see, smell, hear everything, unfiltered. There is a sort of curtain between us, but you have all your injections, do your business, and ask and answer any questions entirely in public. Nothing is private. Suddenly, my life has changed completely. But at least it's life.

Just how incredible that life is hits me late that evening. At around ten o'clock, the night nurse arrives and introduces herself: 'Good evening, I'm Barbara, the night nurse. Is there anything I can do for you?' I pluck up courage: 'Barbara, I hardly dare ask. But I could murder a beer.' Barbara: 'There's a slight problem with that.' Of course, I think, I'm in intensive care; they're hardly going to have any beer. What an idiot. 'A slight problem', Barbara says. 'I've only got Schultheiss.'

For those unfamiliar with Berlin: Schultheiss really isn't a great beer. But that's Berlin humour for you – the original, deadpan verbal wit that catches you out every time. Five minutes later, Barbara brings me a bottle of Schultheiss, ice cold, beads of condensation forming on the glass. I ask Barbara to marry me, which she declines. On the day I survive a heart attack, I end up drinking a beer in the intensive care ward. My new definition of happiness.

I should take this opportunity to say that I have never in my life met a more caring, smarter or wittier set of people than the nurses and doctors in the intensive care unit. I was amazed at how attentive they were to even the most trying of patients (the second old lady who ended up next to me was a nightmare for those around her), the calm, thorough way they went about all their tasks – some of which are really not nice – and the priceless exchanges I had with them. I will spare you the defecation stories, but suffice to say that even something you can't imagine being anything other than humiliating can be quite hilarious when enacted like a theatrical performance.

In short, from auxiliary nurse to senior consultant, they were all sensational. And at no point did any of these wonderful human beings ever make you feel you were being a nuisance. Even when that's exactly how you do feel: useless, dependent, with nothing to offer, only needs to be tended to. One phrase I'll never forget was 'Don't be brave!', said to me by the senior consultant, Dr Opitz, and something of a mantra among cardiologists.

For the record, I made a solemn vow after those two days in intensive care: if I ever find myself in a public situation where some idiot starts ranting about how nothing works in in this country and how everything is run by mindless incompetents, I will stand up and, without ceremony, punch him on the nose. I swear. I owe it to those people. Thank you, all of you! (And if a similar fate should befall you, dear reader, and you happen to be in Berlin, take a tip from me: tell the paramedics to take you to the DRK Westend Clinic!)

What happened next is not particularly interesting: I was fitted with two more stents because – incredibly – all three coronary vessels around my poor heart were clogged, after which I had to be monitored 24/7 with a permanent ECG, before being discharged with a life vest, a piece of kit reminiscent of the explosive vests worn by Islamist assassins. Except that the life vest doesn't kill you: on the contrary, in case of a sudden cardiac arrest, it delivers a hefty electric shock and not only brings you back to life but dials 112 as well. You can imagine what it feels like going to bed in one of these. After four weeks, I was also given a permanent ECG monitor to wear round my neck, which really did make me feel like a cyborg. But finally, once Dr Sonja Diekmann, the best doctor in the world (after all, she saved my life) had meticulously analysed all the data from the vest and ECG, I was allowed to take the whole lot off and feel like my normal self again.

That Dr Diekmann should be 'my' doctor from now on was a no-brainer for me. It's an old native Indian law: once you've saved someone's life, you're responsible for them till the end of time. And she really did save my life. She even contacted her colleagues at the hospital to check whether I had made it through, which they duly confirmed, adding however that 'he [i.e., me] still hasn't the foggiest what a state he's in.' Indeed: while I was feeling on top of the world again since the beer from night nurse Barbara, everyone else knew that, although I had just managed to escape the Devil's clutches, my existence was still hanging by a thread. I had failed to grasp either the precariousness of my position, or the fact that I had a good chance of ending up an invalid. A cardiac arrest leaves a scar on the heart, and the longer it takes for the ambulance to arrive (time is muscle, as cardiologists say), the bigger the scar can get. And because scarred tissue is unable to pump, it reduces cardiac capacity. I thought I was already cured while in hospital – although there were times when a nurse would come rushing into the room in a panic while I was reading my emails or something because the monitor showed my heart rhythm to be out of sync. I found it all a bit over the top. It's amazing how little we are willing to hear and take on board about ourselves and our own lives, especially when the news isn't good. It's the old selective-attention thing. The bad stuff just doesn't get through: heaven forbid!

Bit of background: I hadn't suffered from any heart problems before; my internist had never said or asked anything to that effect (probably negligently); I knew of no risk factors (apart from having been a chain smoker until 15 years previously); and the symptoms that had eventually driven me to my life-saving cardiologist weren't pains, no pressure in my chest, nothing I could identify. The attack was as unexpected as a flowerpot falling on your head from an upper-storey windowsill. Any normal person would dial 112 rather than googling the address of the nearest cardiology centre. But then not every normal person ends up with a doctor who is as quick and efficient as the World's Best Doctor. Several members of the hospital staff assured me that without her lightning reaction, I probably wouldn't have survived. I owe her my life.

Today, some ten months later, I feel great. I still take a cocktail of drugs, but a final examination involving the delightful experience of a cardiac stress MRI yielded an astonishing result: I now have a 'slightly reduced' heart function, which means I won't be climbing Kilimanjaro in a hurry but, that apart, I can do anything – exercise, drink wine, go walking, whatever. A case of incredibly good luck, and incredibly good care. I came away with a deep sense of gratitude. I never wanted to climb Kilimanjaro anyway.

Over the course of my life I have had two serious sports injuries, driven an old VW Beetle into a tree on black ice, survived a motorcycling accident and suffered such a bad fall from a bicycle that I woke up in hospital with no memory of what had happened. Despite this – or perhaps because of it – I thought I was immortal. Until 22 April 2020. On that day, I lost all illusions of immortality. Or rather, soon afterwards, as my cerebral system slowly began to readjust to reality.

Since then, I no longer believe that all human beings must die except me. OK, I have a narcissistic personality, and people who are more normal than me may not believe as firmly in their immortality as I did. But somehow we can't help screening negative information according to the extent to which it might affect us, and every chalice that passes from us confirms us in the hope of being spared. Tolstoy caricatures this trait inimitably in his novella *The Death of Ivan Ilyich* when he describes how news of Ivan Ilyich's death is received by his colleagues: 'Besides considerations as to the possible transfers and promotions likely to result from Ivan Ilyich's death, the mere fact of the death of a near acquaintance aroused, as usual, in all who heard of it the complacent feeling that, "it is he who is dead and not I." Each one thought or felt, "Well, he's dead but I'm alive!"'[22]

And however futile the attempt to suppress the knowledge of our own mortality, we still continue to do it with avidity. Or most of us, at least. Again, this stems from the fact that our culture has no concept of finitude, which is why society is as loath to accept it as the individual is to accept the reality of their own death. We live our lives as if we will never die. Hence the fact that such absurd inventions as 'lifelong learning' (what, pray, is the point of that?) are considered natural and normal. And hence the existence of the cult of youth, with its 'best agers', anti-wrinkle creams, fitness regimes and hyperactive pensioners – at least in modern societies, which are also invariably the rich ones where people can afford such luxuries. We are engaged in an almost manic search for potential ways to disable the biological laws governing the ageing of organisms, and the more often wiry and smooth-skinned septuagenarians go on about how much they are looking forward to their next half-marathon, the crazier it all seems to me. None of this can do anything to prevent the inevitable end.

An experience like mine – psychologists call it a 'critical life event' – also has a fundamental impact on the life you are lucky enough to lead thereafter. Nowadays, I am even positive about bad weather and no longer get so exercised about the bigger stuff going on around me, or at least I don't take it personally. My willingness to read every email, too, has greatly diminished. At the same time, other things have become more important, such as the friendships that proved so resilient – quite wonderful, in fact – during my critical life event. Suddenly, people I hadn't even thought of as particularly close turned out to be extremely empathetic and helpful; some of them phoned me every day just to ask how I was. Others proved a dead loss in that respect – a fact I don't find sad, but instructive. As long as nothing terrible happens, we live our normal lives in a kind of rehearsal mode, on the assumption that it will be ages before the play is actually performed. But a disease like the one I was fortunate enough to survive is not a rehearsal, it's the play itself. That's when you find out who your best co-actors are. I'm with Henning Mankell's fictional police inspector Kurt Wallander on that one: whenever his team has been led up a blind alley, his habitual response is 'So now we know.' Exactly: once something has proved unreliable, you have learnt something. Much more so than if you had simply believed you could rely on it when it came to the crunch. Until then, it is mere conjecture.

As I say, I have lost my illusions of immortality. And just as well. Because the awareness that my life is finite – and, moreover, could end at any moment – has a huge influence on what I do with it. Do I go on living in anticipation of what will happen one day (fair enough in the case of a sixteen-year-old, but surely a bit absurd for someone over sixty)? Do I go on believing I can simply try on people like clothes (to bend a phrase from Max Frisch)? Is there any point in indulging my vanity if no one finds me attractive any longer? Are there training exercises to prepare you for the finiteness of life? Could the awareness of our own mortality possibly hold not terror, but beauty?

And wouldn't it – to pan back from my own case to society at large – be a much better and no doubt pleasanter way to respond to our ecological challenges if we accepted them as phenomena of finitude and finally developed stopping strategies, instead of ploughing on in a perpetual illusion of boundlessness and optimizing what we ought in fact to give up?

Residues of the past

Despite my remark that death has been privatized in the modern age and that modern culture shuns all thought of finitude like the Devil avoids holy water, we still find numerous residues of arational thinking in our contemporary world: 'Just as gigantic eddies of plastic waste have recently formed on the oceans, whose biological degradation will take centuries, if not millennia, so we might imagine eddies of god-residue having formed (albeit less obtrusively) on the oceans of the soul. Their detoxification and recycling is theologically, ethnologically, psychologically, culturally, historically and aesthetically unfinished.'[23]

Examples of such 'god-residues' occur whenever we talk about 'fate', or when something happens to someone for no apparent reason, or when people favour homeopathy over conventional medicine, or when you wish on a shooting star. I am reminded here of an anecdote about Niels Bohr, the Nobel Prize-winning inventor of the atomic model, and his habit of hanging a horseshoe above his laboratory door. When asked by an incredulous visitor if he was superstitious, Bohr is reputed to have replied: 'Of course not, but I am told it works even if you don't believe in it.' This is more or less how I regard astrology or telepathic phenomena: it's probably baloney, but you never know.

And between you and me, aren't Big Bang or black hole theories at least as metaphysical as the idea that the constellation of the stars at the time of my birth could have an influence on my life? Is the CERN Hadron Collider – the 27-kilometre-long particle accelerator buried 100 metres underground which is keeping 15,000–20,000 scientists busy at an annual cost of a billion euros – any more rational than cult rituals for summoning rain or a good harvest? True, that money allowed scientists to prove in real life (or something like it) the existence (theoretically established back in the 1960s) of the Higgs particle – a discovery recognized with the 2013 Nobel Prize. But is that really so much better than believing in magic? Or what about the billions being ploughed into the absurd nuclear fusion reactor ITER? In this case, scientists are now investing more creativity in the justification of further billions than in the patently futile further research into the thing itself, which is obviously never going to work. This is the modern technological equivalent to the art installations of a Panamarenko or a Jean Tinguely: all very clever, but it won't fly.

Again, what kind of rationality underlies the ceaseless attempt to adhere manically to a political, non-scientific value like the notorious 1.5° target, even though the criteria for achieving it are so numerous as to render the project utterly illusory – or is it rational to believe that the global economy will adjust within a few years to the point of making peace with the climate? Or to claim – surely the ultimate absurdity – that churning out electric cars will protect the climate? There is far more rationality in the suggestion of one young car mechanic that we should go on repairing and maintaining existing vehicles and using them as taxis and car shares until the energy and raw materials invested in them are finally exhausted; instead, governments grant incentives to buy new ones.

A most peculiar response to the dissonance arising from our attempt to continue with a cultural model at all costs even when it comes up against objective limits – namely the reality of finitude – is the replacement of actions with targets. Only then is the 1.5° figure system compliant: shifting the problem from the present to the future allows us to organize conferences, negotiate sub-targets, support the automotive industry, agree to phase out coal 15 years later or earlier and so on. During the negotiations of the 'Jamaica' coalition following the German federal election of 2017 (so called because of the party colours), the Green contingent was – so I was told – astonished at how readily the CDU agreed to ambitious climate goals. The difficulty came when they wanted to talk about the imperatives these future goals created for present political action. This, apparently, was a step too far. And when the German Constitutional Court passed a law on 29 April 2021 committing the government to protecting the freedom of future generations by taking prompt action on environmental and climate problems, it responded in record time: by setting new targets.

Perhaps cultural historians of the twenty-first century will look back with amusement on this shift from action to target setting – or perhaps not. In the end, the formulation of climate targets is just a more elegant version of the classic lie that enables us to plough on in the same direction in defiance of new and better information. In other words, the very act of setting

Fig. 1.6: Panamarenko's *Aeromodeller*: learning to fly

a target blocks our path to achieving it. Because it perpetuates the fallacy that future problems are problems to be solved in future.

As we can see, the attempt to pursue a plainly misguided model of civilization at any price and with every conceivable argument requires a large dose of magical thinking. This has little to do with reason, let alone scientific rationalism – and note here that the justification for any given research project invariably comes from outside the scientific community: from industry, society or politics, yes, but never from pure reason.

This non-scientific rationale for scientific activity not only explains the intriguing rise and fall in popularity of individual disciplines but also the strong element of irrationality that still survives in most of us, even in the 'age of reason'. And the deeper cause is probably our inability to fully decode the world around us (scientists would instantly correct that sentence by adding the word 'yet'). Karl Popper highlighted this attitude in his theory of epistemology when he posited that the more we learn, the more we realize how much we don't know. Too true: the logical consequence is an ever more complex knowledge of, to quote Faust, 'whatever holds/ The world together in its inmost folds' – not to mention an almighty work generation scheme for scientists. It is no coincidence that presentations and papers invariably end with the words 'more research needed'. Research, that is, in the existing direction of travel.

This points to an irreconcilable conflict arising from the embeddedness of the social subsystem known as science in the prevailing interests, power relations and self-image of a culture to which scientists themselves will inevitably always belong. 'No one . . . who shares a delusion ever recognizes it as such', said Sigmund Freud, and our collective world view is thus bound by the limits of our cultural perception and interpretative models. Hence we think of the brain as a computer, or invent the image of the *Homo economicus* and build the world around it.

Be that as it may. But the specific conflict in the case of science stems from the fact that this particular subsystem claims to provide reliable knowledge thanks to exact methods and precisely defined 'quality criteria'. Such an approach certainly makes sense, as the COVID epidemic has just demonstrated, as scientific knowledge can only drive rational action against a virus once we know how it spreads. Unfortunately, however, the same process can also drive *irrational* action, when that knowledge leads to things like race theory and eugenics, and seeks to eradicate those deemed 'unworthy of life' or 'social deviants'. In both cases, non-scientific values and policies form the usage context for properly conducted science, with fundamentally different results. This simple fact is, incidentally, the reason why science-based policy is always totalitarian.[24]

Besides, the scientific community often overlooks the fact that the data, discoveries and insights it provides can end up being used in a social context which the responsible researchers could never have imagined. Thus the endless stream of bad news from climate scientists, such as the melting of glaciers or Arctic ice, doesn't necessarily lead people to change their behaviour for the good – quite the opposite. It is perfectly possible for a person to believe the alarming findings of Hans-Joachim Schellnhuber and colleagues at the Potsdam Institute for Climate Research beyond all doubt and be sincerely shocked at the foreseeable consequences of unchecked climate change, yet at the same time book a long-haul flight to the Maldives on the basis that they will one day be submerged by rising sea levels and no longer accessible.

If it hadn't been for climate research, would the cruise company Hurtigruten have even thought of the lucrative idea of 'on-board science' cruises in the Antarctic and elsewhere? One brochure for a South Pole trip reads:

> Next, we head for the legendary Drake Passage. During our lecture series, you'll be given lots of information on the fabulous fauna and history of the Antarctic. We will also advise you on how to make your visit as sustainable as possible. By participating in the Citizen Science Programs, you will be helping us to collect data for the latest scientific research.

Citizen Science is a scheme whereby people gather data from their environment – such as bird or insect counts – for scientific purposes and make them available to the research community. On these Antarctic cruises, Citizen Science gives people the illusion that they are doing something meaningful against global warming by travelling on a pleasure boat and contributing to the destruction of the natural environment. This is another instance of the magical thinking that tells us it's OK to do the wrong thing if you do it with the right intentions. If only.

The German mining, chemicals and energy workers' union IGBCE, for instance, constitutes one of the country's biggest obstacles to sustainability. Take this statement from a Kafkaesque position paper it has produced on the phase-out of coal: 'It is already the case that many industrially manufactured products have a positive CO_2 balance. The amounts of CO_2 avoided by their use are greater than those generated during their production. This approach is more constructive than considering the resource consumption of industrial production processes in isolation.'[25] In other words, boost production to reduce CO_2! Here, in all its intellectual brilliance, is a prime example of how arguments are taken from climate science and subverted into absurdity.

Taking this to its logical conclusion, you could say that, without alarmist reports from climate scientists, there would be no cruises to the Antarctic, Elon Musk wouldn't be building a car factory in eastern Germany and politicians wouldn't be promoting the greening of industrial society on the basis that it brings economic advances. All these are counterintuitive responses to the message that we are facing a survival problem in the twenty-first century. But they are only the tip of the iceberg.

Stories of conspicuous consumption[26]

On 12 September 2017, Germany's *Bild* newspaper ran a full-page feature entitled 'My crazy round-the-world trip'. In it, the journalist Michael Quandt reported that he had visited 'four continents and eight cities' in just five days, clocking up nearly 25,000 air miles (or around 40,000 kilometres) in the process – and because he had flown economy class, the whole thing had cost just 1,827 euros. His report is peppered with details of excursions – dromedary rides in Dubai and eating shave ice on Waikiki Beach, complete with the obligatory Instagram photos

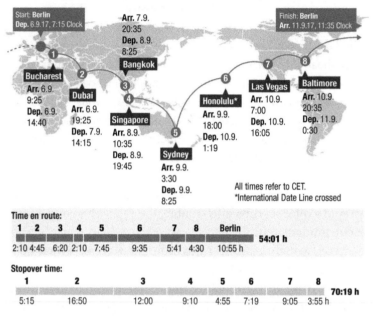

The crazy 124-hour round-the-world trip
BILD reporter visits 8 cities on 4 continents – for just 1827 euros!

Fig. 1.7:   *Bild* report: 25,000 air miles in five days

to prove it. We hear about the rooftop bar Level 43 in Dubai, the Sampeng Night Market in Bangkok, the 'cool infinity pool on the 57th floor of Marina Bay Sands' in Singapore and so on. All the Insta-friendly tourist highlights you see advertised in brochures are ticked off and documented. And what for? 'The indescribably heady feeling of having seen so much of the world for so little money.'

Another full-page article in the 'Technology and Motoring' section of the *Frankfurter Allgemeine Zeitung*, dated 14 May 2019, reports on so-called explorer ships, the new 'jewel in the crown of the yacht building industry'. These are designed for active, adventurous and extremely rich individuals keen to venture into unknown territories such as the Arctic. The ships have much to offer such people:

The SeaXplorer 75 will provide suites for up to twelve passengers. The first model, measuring exactly 76.9 metres by 14 metres wide, is currently under construction. The buyer, a passionate skier, surfer and diver, will have an arsenal of sport and leisure equipment on board: surfing gear, diving chamber, dive boat, ski room complete with avalanche safety equipment, two snowmobiles, four jet skis, a submarine, lifeboat, premium tender and two outboard dinghies. The two Airbus ACH 125 helicopters are transported from the double hangar below deck to the certified helideck by a lift measuring a good 11 metres. Maximum take-off weight 4,000 kilos.

Why two helicopters?, you may ask. Simple: if one of the intrepid explorers runs into trouble, the other can come to the rescue immediately.

These two stories reflect the different ways in which people's 'share of the world' is steadily increasing according to income. This term, coined by the sociologist Hartmut Rosa, aptly describes a feature of the modern age whereby growing wealth and technological innovation allow the individual to access more and more of the world. Only a century ago, venturing no further than your own village or at most the next largest town was nothing unusual; nowadays, it would be a total aberration. Until the first half of the twentieth century, only soldiers in the field got to travel the world; everyone else – apart from a few very rich people – spent their whole lives at home. It was only after the Second World War that mass tourism got going in Germany, initially to the classic dream destination of Italy, and subsequently, according to budget, to Spain, Tunisia, Turkey and so on. Although predated by the subsidized workers' holidays (*Kraft durch Freude*) of the Nazi era, this new phenomenon took off in earnest with the Economic Miracle and has never looked back. The example of the *Bild* reporter clearly shows that even round-the-world trips are no longer the exclusive preserve of the upper classes – nowadays, you can span the globe for 1,827 euros.

All of which is bad news for the super-rich. After all, increasing one's share of the world is an aspect of status consumption, and if everybody does it, it loses its kudos. So the logical next step is to up the game – with 'explorer' ships. But – as a glance at the travel sections of the print media reveals – the mass market is never far behind, hence the Hurtigruten trips to the Antarctic. You can even go helicopter skiing in Georgia.

Why the digression? First, expanding luxury consumption becomes all the more destructive when it develops into the mass consumption that lies at the root of our current environmental problems and changing climate. It goes without saying that the owner of the Explorer 75 is an environmental super-destroyer, but the damage done by millions of budget tourists following in his wake is many times worse. Second – and more pertinently to the following observations – I have cited the *Bild* and *FAZ* stories because they present the concept of increasing world share as desirable and worthy of imitation.

Such 'imperial lifestyles', as Ulrich Brand and Markus Wissen have aptly branded this practice of world appropriation, are thus constantly championed as something to be aspired to without so much as a nod to half a century of environmental campaigning. The growth in global consumption continues to be presented positively in media, advertising, business and political circles, and is subsidized and promoted accordingly. Most people are no more likely to regard a luxury yacht as an environmental nightmare or even an anachronism than they are monstrous Chelsea tractors, wall-to-wall widescreen TVs or massive farmhouse kitchens that no one ever cooks in. On the contrary, the most common response to such things is 'I want one too'.

And why wouldn't they? After all, traditional economics, like traditional politics, continues to assume that growth is not only economically necessary but also essential for a stable society. If we were to replace the term 'growth' consistently with 'higher consumption', the underlying problem would immediately become a little clearer. Because it is this logic of ever-increasing global consumption that has got the modern, twentieth-century model of civilization into such deep water.

Consequently, anyone attempting to motivate people in hyper-consumerist societies like Germany to act in a sustainable, climate-friendly manner is forced to recognize that their efforts are up against strong, if not overwhelming, competition from stories like the above. The dominance of conspicuous consumption stories of the Explorer type is all-encompassing, as a glance at the travel sections of the print media or our 24/7 exposure to web advertising shows. As such, it seems somewhat presumptuous to expect calls for moderation or 'sufficiency' to be seen as appealing alternatives and thus hope to win fans to one's cause. After all, what seventeen-year-old is interested in 'moderation'?

Similarly misguided is the attempt to achieve improvement through awareness raising. Awareness is only loosely linked to behaviour, as is immediately apparent if you compare the results of surveys on environmental and climate anxiety with the radical increase in environmental consumption over the past decades. The rise in environmental awareness has been accompanied by a continuous rise in GDP, meaning that more resources have had to be exploited and processed using more energy, more goods have been exported and shipped around the world, and more emissions and waste have been generated – to the point that dead mass now exceeds biomass. And this trajectory remains unbroken. To quote Raj Patel and Jason Moore, 'Every global factory needs a global farm.'[27] In their book *A History of the World in Seven Cheap Things*, they point to a fundamental, but for the most part intentionally overlooked, fact: 'Industrial, technological and service enterprises rely on the extraction of work and cheap nature to thrive. The apps on your iPhone, designed in Cupertino, California, might have been coded by self-exploiting independent software engineers, and the phone itself assembled in draconian workplaces in China, and run on minerals extracted in inhumane conditions in the Congo.'[28]

The way society deals with these obvious contradictions is to declare – with almost farcical disingenuousness – the generation of more wealth a necessary precondition for doing something for the environment or for the workers on the ground. Or to take the greenwashing of conventional products to such lengths that outsized hybrid SUVs or gas-powered cruise ships are presented as 'climate-friendly'. The fact that the only sustainable alternative to such products is their complete removal from the face of the earth is ignored. But that's how capitalism works: fluid enough to incorporate into the economy those elements that were originally critical of it. Even environmental awareness can be turned into a product.

On an individual level, too, it is extremely easy to overcome the residual misgivings we feel when we do things that are *actually* wrong. Reasons can always be found, and they cost nothing. Human beings have no problem at all integrating the most blatant contradictions into their day-to-day lives. The idea that humans strive for consistency has found its way into our collective imagination from moral philosophy and theology, but it is completely untrue. People behave quite differently in different situations – whether at work, on the sports field, within the family or among friends – depending on the relevant role expectations. The functional differentiation of societies based on the division of labour has given rise to an extremely flexible subject type that takes in its stride the changing and often highly contradictory demands of its various roles in the context of family, work, extracurricular activities, friendships and so on. The American sociologist Erving Goffman devoted his whole career to demonstrating that people in modern societies show huge situational variation in their perception, interpretation and behaviour, and that they have no difficulty in distancing themselves in one role from norms they may conform to in another ('Are you asking me as a politician or as a private individual?'). In all but borderline pathological cases, it is nonsense to attribute human actions to non-situational motives. On the contrary, modern societies have no place for normopaths. Nowadays, anyone who always responds in the same way whatever the situation is likely to end up in a psychiatric ward.

The flexible individual is not a pathological variant of an essentially fixed one: they are a product of the socialization processes and educational institutions of modern societies, which need them to be that way in order to function. People are expected to be flexible, agile and open to lifelong learning; if possible, they should be quick, alert and creative. Yet at the same time they must be compliant, and kindly refrain from thinking for themselves.

Contrary to popular perception, moral convictions do not drive behaviour: they merely help us find suitable justifications for aligning a wrong deed with the right intention. The universal adverb for this purpose is 'actually'. The very existence of this curious word suggests that the contradiction between what we say and what we do is a fact of everyday life. Its meaning has shifted over time from 'fundamentally' to 'I know I ought to do this, but I have reasons for not doing so.' With such a word at our disposal, we needn't be bound by consistency.

Added to this is the fact that our everyday behaviour is largely driven by routines and habits. Only rarely do our actions stem from conscious decisions: the vast majority are predetermined by the material and cultural conditions that make up the world we inhabit. As we have seen, the world we grow up in is accepted as a given. Its texture is formed by the cultural and social foundation of our existence, the symbolic universe. And it is precisely because they are hardly ever the object of conscious reflection that the rules of that universe have such power to define reality. What you don't know, you can't criticize or call into doubt.

The social rules of everyday life are by no means the only unconscious source of our attitudes and expectations, however. Modern societies in particular are constructed around institutional regulations and infrastructures of all kinds. The 'assumptive world' we inhabit (to use Alfred Schütz's term) not only shapes our perceptions and interpretations (such as 'we don't eat dogs') but imposes cultural obligations on us and makes connections that are also unconscious. All cultures equip their members with behavioural, expectational and emotional standards whose very effectiveness derives from the fact that, for the most part, they have never had to be accounted for. Consequently, efforts to change those standards achieve absolutely nothing if they only focus on the cognitive level – that is, where something is consciously accessible to experience. Because habitus operates below the threshold of consciousness, it is generally fruitless to appeal to 'insight' and 'reason'. In Kantian terms, the world operates only in the narrow window occupied by our waking consciousness. And insight doesn't usually percolate through to behaviour because behaviour is not based on insight.

Socio-psychologically significant facts of this kind bring bad news – from climate science, for instance – into a curious conflict with lived reality. Because every piece of data, every diagram, every impassioned speech by a Mojib Latif or a Hans Joachim Schellnhuber is interpreted as a threat to our familiar way of life. The more seriously these are taken, the less indifferent the apparent response. Paradoxically, however, bad news from scientists can have the opposite effect to that intended: fear and loss aversion do not result in a change in lifestyles and cultural models, but to an even stronger adherence to them. Better make the most of things while you can! How else do we explain the fact that awareness of climate change has not led to smaller, more economical cars but to ever larger

Fig. 1.8:　A riddle for posterity?

gas guzzlers? The engine power of newly registered vehicles has not diminished but steadily increased, as has their average weight. Whereas automotive designers in the eighties used to conceal the exhaust coyly behind the bumper for instance, they now flaunt it in huge (and functionally superfluous) pipes, while the front design is more aggressive than at any time in the past hundred years, and the spatial and resource footprint of vehicles boundless.

The same goes for modern forms of tourism which, in all their many varieties from e-mountain biking to Arctic cruises, have become more expansive and escapist than ever before. In psychospeak: the data-supported call to change our hyper-consumerist lifestyle generates reactance. Or, in plain English: people do exactly the opposite of what was intended and rush to consume even more. Surprise, surprise!

Only those who are part of the operating system we call science believe, due to their *déformation professionnelle*, that behaviour is driven by knowledge; others are more realistic and assume that interests, power, routine, indifference and other factors are probably more influential than knowledge. Not to mention stupidity.

Therefore, it is high time to stop the warnings and exhortations. Not just because they have long been priced into the habits and careers of those who have been exposed to the same five-minutes-to-midnight warnings for decades – in many cases a lifetime – without the slightest positive change being observable in our economic and social operating system. But also because the appetite for global consumption is clearly growing, not diminishing, in proportion to the urgency of those warnings.

Scaring Mr Ochs

There is an unfortunate convergence of two factors here which are typical of the imperial lifestyle. First, everything the world has to offer appears to be available only to those who can afford it (not for nothing do we talk about 'costing the earth'); and, second, pointing out the limits of growth instantly invites aggressive reactance. 'I'm not going to let these kids spoil my hard-earned SUV', an evidently incensed Mr Eberhard Ochs wrote to me in response to an article of mine in *Die Zeit* in which I proposed a ban on the vehicles and expressed support for the 'Fridays for Future' protests. The same aggressiveness can be observed in politicians who feel called upon to defend the practices of eating factory-farmed meat or flying on holiday against vegans and anti-aviation campaigners. It is astonishing how much fury the offending 'kids' arouse – after all, they are hardly calling for a revolution, or even the overthrow of the system. All someone has to do is say 'We think there's a limit' for it to be understood as an attack on one's personal lifestyle.

But perhaps such aggressiveness reflects a small seed of doubt about the sustainability of a lifestyle of boundless extravagance. I doubt that a vegan schoolgirl would have had the power to scare a hardened mega-consumer ten or fifteen years ago, yet today we go into panic stations as soon as anyone so much as dares to question any aspect of the universal gravy train. A typical example of the mental and argumentative effort people seem to devote to such rebuttals nowadays comes from the *Frankfurter Allgemeine Zeitung* of 8 October 2019, in which a writer called Tobias Piller mounts a fierce defence of SUVs against what he calls 'envious' detractors, culminating in the following argument: 'SUVs are also equipped with modern technology designed to prevent or lessen the impact of collisions with pedestrians. Should this happen, however, their higher ground clearance means that the person concerned – whether adult or child – may have a higher chance of survival.' In other words, if you're going to be run over, make sure it's by an SUV! Such a rationale gives some sense of the delirium of compulsive adherence to the suchness of the world and the religion of 'Away-from-here'. The lengths people will go to to find even the most tenuous argument demonstrate a secret fear that things can't go on like this for much longer.

To look at it another way: these are the voices of addicts doing their utmost to rationalize an addiction they are unwilling to give up. And they are aided in this by the fact that their addiction is a sign of conformity, not deviance. *Everyone says so!* Our culture has trained us to regard endless escalation as desirable, and we are not ready to surrender the hard-won fruits of that lesson. Under no circumstances. What was it Ivan Illich said? 'When maddening behaviour becomes the standard of a society, people learn to compete for the right to engage in it.'[29]

As long as the expansive cultural model continues to prevail, there can and will be no change of course in favour of sustainable and climate-friendly economic practices and lifestyles. What we are talking about here is not will and imagination, but practices that shape our world and our appropriation and understanding of it. In good old-fashioned Marxist terms, being determines consciousness, not vice versa. If we are to have a realistic chance of tackling the challenges of runaway climate change and all the other equally urgent ecological crises, there are many things we will have to *stop* doing. This cannot be achieved through idealistic awareness raising but only by actively changing the way we do things.

Sympathy for the Devil

Pop music has had many moments of lucidity, and the song 'Sympathy for the Devil' was one of them. This song by Mick Jagger and Keith Richards describes a principle that we see enacted with astonishing regularity throughout history: that of adversity, personified here in the figure who reveals his name at the end. 'Hope you guess my name' is a reference to the old belief that the Devil, Lucifer, evil incarnate, should not be mentioned by name: only then could his power be suppressed.

Nevertheless, as the song recounts, many things happen that strike us as the Devil's work, precisely because they are so successful: how, we may ask, did Hitler manage – in what was, on the whole, an improbable set of circumstances – to seize power, miraculously escape all assassination attempts and only depart from the world stage after the biggest mass slaughter in the history of humankind and the destruction of an entire continent? How did Pol Pot manage to set up an absurd, Stone Age version of communism in Cambodia to which up to a quarter of the population fell victim – and why, at the same time, did German left-wing intellectuals who went on to become professors regard 'democratic Cambodia' as a sign of social progress? Why do so many former revolutionaries and freedom fighters – Robert Mugabe, Daniel Ortega – turn into ruthless despots? Why does the same thing always happen whenever people gain power?

Why – to take a rather more innocuous example – did Al Gore lose the 2000 US election by a grotesque 0.5 per cent of votes in a single federal state, cemented by a Supreme Court decision against a recount? Perhaps we would no longer be talking about the threat of global warming today if a Gore administration had begun putting the necessary measures in place two decades ago and, moreover, spared itself the madness of a futile 'war on terror'. And who knows whether 9/11 would have happened in those circumstances? What if the Chinese freedom movement had coincided with a more moderate Communist Party leadership, like Gorbachev in the Soviet Union, instead of Deng Xiaoping? And how absurd that none other than Gorbachev himself was due to speak in Tian'anmen Square on that fateful day, but his appearance was cancelled because of the student occupation. Sympathy for the Devil.

Why do assassination attempts on people like Martin Luther King, the Kennedys, Olof Palme and Alfred Herrhausen suc-ceed, but not those against Hitler, Stalin and other assholes of world history? Hitler alone survived forty attempts on his life and used this fact for propaganda purposes, as a sign that 'providence' was protecting him at all costs in order to ensure the continuation of his beneficent leadership.

The only philosopher who – as far as I can see – has explored the 'principle of adversity' is, ironically, the 'philosopher of hope', Ernst Bloch. In his last book, *Experimentum Mundi*, he deals with the category of evil: 'The poison of disease, the ever newly disguised and ideologized forms of exploitation and repression culminating in the anonymity of capital, for every thousand wars there are barely ten revolutions, all Reichstag fires succeed so easily'[30] – all these things, writes Bloch, leave us bewildered in the face of 'the as yet inadequately defined concept of adversity in the world'.[31]

Here Bloch develops – alas, only briefly – a remarkable idea: while secularization brought a worldly interpretation of the divine principle and, with Kant, turned it into a reason-led human responsibility, the same thing did not happen in rela-tion to the Devil and belief in the Devil: 'demythologization thus led to a marked disappearance of the object that seemed to be so often encountered in all mythologies of evil. . . . The secularization of the rest . . . did not happen, and little or nothing was accomplished in this respect.'[32]

I find this insight quite spectacular: the Devil hasn't been secularized, but God has. And that is why our secularized society, with its belief in progress, always regards accidents, calamities, catastrophes and terror attacks as a fundamentally alien phenomenon. They are strangely at odds with our progressive modern world, eliciting adjectives such as 'tragic', 'terrible', 'cruel', 'cowardly' and so on. A catastrophe is always a deviation from the norm. Hence the huge frustration when the COVID pandemic turned out to be a long-term affair and politicians attempted to govern largely by metaphor ('light at the end of the tunnel', 'ray of hope on the horizon'). This, too, is a dialectic of the modern age: standards of security and predictability have risen to such an extent in rich societies that our expectations of institutions and politicians have risen accordingly, and our disappointment is thus all the greater when they are not met.

In such cases, an 'investigation' is then immediately demanded, by way of compensation, into the cause of the disaster in question, and the inevitable blame game begins. In our media-dominated society, this response has become almost Pavlovian: as soon as anything goes wrong, members of the political opposition and news-hungry journalists immediately start to salivate at the prospect of the ensuing manhunt.

In the cartoon series *South Park*, there is a superhero called Captain Hindsight. Whenever a fire breaks out in an apartment block or an oil rig is damaged, he flies to the scene to explain the causes of the disaster to the desperate helpers: the houses are built too close together for the fire brigade to move in close with their extinguishers; the roof should have been designed so that a helicopter could land on it and rescue the residents. Having once explained everything, Captain Hindsight then

Fig. 1.9:   Spot the error: Merkel goes Captain Hindsight

takes off again to loud cheers. The building carries on burning, but everyone is happy.

Modern society does not take a systemic view of disaster but regards it as something foreign, alien, extraneous. Nor is there such a thing as 'disasterology'; the sociology of disaster – founded on the notion that disasters are inevitable – centred on a single figure, the brilliant German sociologist Lars Clausen, but has remained extremely marginal as a discipline. As a result, we still have no concept of a gradually unfolding catastrophe whose consequences get worse the later we intervene.

Telling in this respect is our use of the word 'crisis', which is frequently applied to developments from which there can be no return to a prior state. In its original medical sense, however, the term refers to the climax of a problematic development; having once overcome the crisis, the organism returns to its normal, non-critical state (or else dies). When the word is applied to social and political events, it is almost always incorrect: in the case of the 'refugee crisis', for example, it suggests a phenomenon which, though problematic, is only temporary – a far cry from the reality, given the United Nations (UN) Refugee Agency's estimate that, by 2040, approximately 200 million people will be driven from their homes by war, displacement, persecution and climate change. The effects of climate change on refugee numbers are hard to predict because events such as droughts, floods, fires and hurricanes can lead very suddenly to situations that render it impossible for people to survive in their existing environment. Today, there are 80 million on the move – that's not a crisis, but a point along a steadily rising curve. The refugee will be the defining figure of the twenty-first century because survival spaces are finite.

The same goes for climate change which – given the political will – can be slowed down but not reversed. There is no such thing as a climate crisis, only climate change, or – if we want to put it more dramatically – global warming. Just as the effects of climate change, many of which are now acutely visible, are due to greenhouse gas emissions released into the atmosphere 30 years ago, so our present economic metabolism is producing effects that will in turn only be felt a generation later. Unlike in Monopoly, no one gets the chance to return to 'Go'.

Such developments cannot be dealt with appropriately if we call them 'crises'. They demand not just urgent measures to mitigate even worse consequences in future but an expectation of successful adaptation. An example of unsuccessful adaptation is the EU refugee policy, which attempts – in a deeply inhumane and self-damaging manner – to get rid of the problem by getting rid of the refugees. The trouble is that they keep on coming. And we will never deal with climate change if we don't, first, make adaptations in preparation for hotter times to come, just like we do (albeit more slowly for structural reasons) in the case of dam building or forestry management or urban planning; and, second, if we don't do everything humanly possible to bring down and ultimately end CO_2 emissions, paradoxical though this project is, given our continued attachment to an economic system characterized by constant acceleration and the notion of limitlessness (see above).

To take Bloch's approach, we could ask exactly where the forces of adversity lie here: in a fatally warming climate system or in the vested interests of those who are doing their level best to avoid making any concessions to climate protection? I have already talked about the absurdities to which such a policy leads but, more fundamentally, it prevents us from taking a realistic view of the situation because it promotes the idea that we can somehow magically combine action against climate change with continued growth (indeed, Lars Clausen identi-fied 'magicization' as one of the most common responses to disasters). Conversely, if we had a cultural concept or even just a practical sense of finitude, the search for solutions would be forced to take a different direction: then we would no longer be talking about such bizarrely magical notions as 'decarbonizing the economy' while simultaneously making more products from more resources. Instead, we would be seeking to reduce our economic metabolism so that we make fewer products from fewer resources.

In order to pursue this strategy, however, we need – in the words of the philosopher and essayist Günther Anders – to be able to visualize what we are producing. Which brings us back to the issue of dead mass outweighing biomass: who is capable of imagining the resources necessary to reach such a point? It's easy enough to imagine the individual houses or cars or whatever which make up the dead mass, but not the globally orchestrated apparatus necessary for its produc-tion. All the dead labour, all the dead material. This, too, is only noticeable by its absence – as in the COVID epidemic, when it suddenly became clear that things like face masks, PPE, drugs and vaccines are not simply 'out there', but actually 'come from' somewhere. This was something we had never considered before. And why would we when the magic of the hyper-consumerist society lies in the very ahistoricality of the products on the market? The invisibility of our society's economic metabolism is apparent every time we swipe a device that betrays nothing of the mines and factories that produced it, or the container ships that transported it around the world. Or every time we stream films and order goods that seem to have come into the world by similarly magic means – abracadabra, and there they are.

If for whatever reason the DHL van fails to turn up at your door with these items, it messes with your head. Yet the fact that we can normally have everything we want whenever we want it has long since ceased to mess with anyone's head.

Ahistoricality is, incidentally, a principle of adversariality; the Lucifer of the Stones song wanders through history wreaking havoc as he pleases – without preconditions, without reason, without preparation, without preamble. For a culture that believes itself capable of calculating 'probabilities of occurrence', accidents, disasters and unexpected events must remain an exception; if, as in premodern societies, it reckoned consistently with failed harvests, famines, earthquakes and wars, then disaster would be factored into expectations. And only then would culture be able to deal with it.

The absence of a secular incarnation of the Adversary is particularly noticeable in the case of man-made catastrophes such as genocides and mass killings, brutal displacements, mass rape, ethnic cleansing, land grabs, terrorist attacks or large-scale organized crime. In such cases, the category of 'evil' is often bandied around, but what is meant by it and why perfectly normal or even good people see fit to do 'evil' things is hardly ever addressed.

Shouldn't we, like Bloch, take the practical approach and, instead of always starting from the assumption that everything 'ought to' go right, allow for the fact that the very opposite can happen and, historically, does so on a not infrequent basis? Indeed, that – to invoke Lars Clausen again – the occasional disaster is inevitable? And not because it

was subjectively willed by someone – be it from convic-
tion, maleducation or childhood trauma – but because, for
example, it appeared logical, necessary or natural within the
cultural model inhabited by that person (say, an ordinary
shoemaker or dentist serving as a reserve policeman) to participate in something like the systematic shooting of Jews.
Such a deed needs no motive, just the simple fact of being in
a social situation and belonging to a social group that makes
one's participation appear necessary and indicative of solidarity. In this way, perfectly normal people can become mass
murderers; as I attempted to show in a study years ago, they
don't need to be psychopaths – in fact, psychopaths are often
more likely to hinder the smooth execution of mass murder
because their behaviour cannot be predicted or controlled.[33]
Does anyone really believe that the teams of Chinese guards
policing, commanding, controlling and bullying the Uigurs at
the re-education camps in Xinjiang are 'evil' people? Nor do
they need to be: all they need is regular wages, good working
conditions and, if the state is lucky, a belief that it is right to
treat the Uigurs that way. And why should they doubt their
own normality when it is confirmed by everyone else in their
normal society – and not even the famous global community
expresses any doubt, favouring trade with China over the
rejection of slavery and genocide?

So where exactly are the forces of adversity? In the psychology of our modern culture, there are only problems that have
not yet been solved or situations where something is deemed,
Captain Hindsight-style, to have gone wrong. The problems
will be solved as soon as we have gathered all the necessary
knowledge, technology and funding and eliminated all sources
of error. The guys from Silicon Valley are past masters at this:
artificial intelligence, they promise, will *solve all the world's
problems*, eliminate all diseases, save the environment and so
on and so forth. What this solutionist approach doesn't take
into account, however, is that man-made history is not a fixed

test set-up with a few bugs here and there, but a process with a plethora of feedback loops, idiosyncrasies, 'black swans' and other complicating factors.

And it doesn't even begin to consider that, as natural beings, we are dependent upon physical and biological factors that have to be factored into the solution. Volcanic eruptions, earthquakes, tsunamis, cyclones, pandemics and the like will continue to happen, however awesome the powers of artificial intelligence, and their consequences can only be mitigated provided there is sufficient social intelligence to invest money and knowledge in disaster prevention. And provided there are functioning health systems and functioning infrastructures, without which, incidentally, even the smartest AI would no longer work, as a prolonged power cut would very soon render it one hundred per cent stupid. At least human beings can still think when faced with catastrophe and apply themselves to finding a way out.

But to return to our question: how do we explain adversity? It arises from the simple fact that, as natural beings, we are mortal and, in the unfortunate event of a disaster, will still die even if we have done everything right *up to that point* – gone to school like good children, got an education, donated to Greenpeace and always taken care with our appearance. None of which is any help when something bad happens. Disasters are the test case for enlightenment: only then can we tell what good all our knowledge and problem-solving abilities are. If we're lucky, a great deal; if we're unlucky, none at all.

The earth we live on, the air we breathe, the wind that blows on us, the rain that soaks us, plants, animals, rocks: all this is not a stage for us to perform on or some kind of 3D photo-graphic wallpaper providing a backdrop to our actions, but the variable and ultimately unpredictable constellation that makes our life possible or, conversely, destroys it. This can indeed be said to have an element of the diabolic in that it pays no heed to categories such as justice or the balance of interests. Take the current virus, for example: it attacks people all over the world quite indiscriminately, and it mutates as fast as the vaccines – already developed at record speed – can keep it at bay. This consciousnessless, brainless being is the tortoise to our hare, crying not only 'I'm the winner!' but 'That'll teach you, smart-asses!' Nor should we forget that zoonoses are also man-made, caused by human activity impinging on habitat and forcing animals and humans to live – to their mutual detriment – in closer proximity to one another. Here, again, we see how the principle of adversity is part of the dynamic of the earth system, not something that can ever be conquered. Strategies for dealing with it are more likely to lie in risk assessment and socio-technical measures. You can't abolish disasters.

There is another aspect of adversity, too, that is much more complicated to define. It is in the nature of the human condition that our actions often have unexpected consequences because they affect individuals, social groups, organizations and institutions that then interpret those actions, draw conclusions from them and so generate a new reality. This highly complex state of affairs is encapsulated by two pithy statements: the consequences of yesterday's actions are the conditions for today's actions (Johan Goudsblom), and 'if men define situations as real, they are real in their consequences' (William Thomas). Humans exist within webs of relationships of varying size and complexity, and everyone within those webs interprets things and makes decisions based on their interpretations. This is not a purely rational process, however, as those decisions can be affected by an indefinite number of factors: power relationships, interests, emotional needs – in short, everything that matters to human beings. Much of this happens implicitly and unconsciously, yet it often does more to determine the outcomes of actions than conscious considerations.

In other words, unlike physical events for example, societal events and their outcomes in particular need to be understood not causally but in the context of inter-human relationships.

And they take place in time, speeding up or slowing down, escalating or stopping short. Which, crucially, brings us back to the point I made at the beginning of this book: that the behaviour of such relationship webs can take a wrong turn and – perhaps even with the best intentions – become self-destructive. And while it is hard enough to confidently predict the actions of an individual, it's far harder in the case of groups or whole societies. Consequently, any reasonably accurate forecast will be either banal or limited to an abstract category ('If there were an election next week . . .'). As a rule, such forecasts are formulated – as in so-called trend research – based on a knowledge of what people would like to see happen in the short term. Economic researchers have made an alchemistic art of announcing the growth for the next quarter and simply adjusting their forecast if things turn out differently. (The fact that they have been getting away with this without any real loss of credibility is another clear sign that we most certainly do not live in a 'knowledge society'.)

But back to the adversity principle: in the interests of a truly enlightened engagement with the world, it would be sensible, 250 years on from Kant, to recognize that, alongside the progress we imagine to be infinite, there is also its opposite – retrogression – or its nullification, namely disaster, the collapse of civilization. To do so would be an essential first step towards recognizing and dealing with the central problem of the twenty-first century and its numerous ancillary problems: global warming, mass migration, species extinction, pandemics and everything else that is glibly described as a 'crisis'.

No, we must learn that these are not crises but unfolding chains of events from which there can be no return to a status quo ante. In order to understand such developments, and above all to deal with them in a manner conducive to our survival, we need to take a realistic view, which also includes the awareness that *all will not be well again* afterwards. The disasters we are facing in the twenty-first century are problems of finitude: in places where the climate heats up beyond a certain threshold, human life is no longer possible. Where this is the case, people flee. Where resources are grown and mined without regard for plants and

Fig. 1.10:   'Onwards!' Wishful thinking, Mr Marcuse?

animal life, species go extinct. And where they go extinct, food chains are disrupted and the dying becomes cumulative. All this can only be described as 'complex' and 'impenetrable' if we have no concept of finitude. If we turn the tables and consider things from the standpoint of finitude, all the looming man-made disasters of the twenty-first century become perfectly logical. And hence to my question: what if we fail?

Humanity unbound

We have already made several references to the fact that culture is not something purely external but is also ingrained in our mentality, our psyche, our self-image. So how did these notions of boundlessness and the infinity of life and its metabolism – notions that were certainly not entertained by premodern man – come about? The answer lies in the historical constellation of early industrialization, philosophical Enlightenment, Protestant accountability culture and bookkeeping which, over a couple of centuries, have shaped the mentalities and identity-formation processes that continue to dominate our perception of ourselves and the world, our interpretive paradigms and life goals to this day.[34]

The keyword here is individualization – the notion that one can and should organize one's own life. The *Bildungsroman*, or 'coming of age' novel, which appeared around the turn of the eighteenth century with Goethe's *Wilhelm Meister* (1796) and Karl Philipp Moritz's *Anton Reiser* (1790), is a testimony to the fact that one's life is not set in stone but should be understood as a process of self-education. As noted, however, this didn't just mean liberation from external constraints: hand in hand with the new freedom came hitherto unknown organizational imperatives and pressures. Categories such as self-responsibility, discipline and will become important for individuals growing up in a culture where it is not only possible to make something of oneself, but indeed necessary. This is what the *Bildungsroman* is all about.

And just as the labourer liberated from feudal constraints is free to work where he chooses, so he is also free, in Marx's words, to 'bring his own hide to market', meaning that he is simultaneously released from the certainties of an unfree existence. 'From this perspective, the historical process of individualization means that a person is no longer identified by a social position or membership of a social unit, but by his own life agenda.'[35] Here, then, is an early form of what we would call a life story, a career, an autobiography.

In the premodern age, life was a period of time over which one had little control, punctuated by such things as communions, weddings and the deaths of family members. With the freedom to forge one's own path, however, came the duty to demonstrate 'a life's work on earth'.[36] And with that duty came a constant need for orientation and self-realization. Wilhelm von Humboldt expressed this as the necessity to 'absorb as much of the world as possible' – and so the norm was born whereby we constantly strive to increase our own share of the world. This same norm, however, led to an ever-growing pressure to see oneself and one's own life in economic terms.

In the modern age, we are at liberty to 'lead' that life, successfully or otherwise, and that demands control, moderation and self-scrutiny. 'As much of the world as possible' – that emphatic phrase already foreshadows the bourgeois capitalist value system of 'better, further, faster', the destination of 'Away-from-here', but turned inwards: thus the self becomes a continuous development process with fixed stages and objectives, so that biographical success – indeed, the balance sheet of life itself – becomes measurable.

The 'economic man' that we know today, as the philosopher Joseph Vogl argues, is characterized by the fact that he has to document his own developmental progress within a precise and increasingly systematized universe of checks, books and balances, and account for it both inwardly and outwardly. This perpetually self-scrutinizing economic man first appears – as Max Weber noted in his famous study *The Protestant Ethic and the Spirit of Capitalism* – in the shape of the typical bourgeois entrepreneur or 'professional' who records every business transaction with minute precision and is constantly on the lookout for ways of optimizing his methods and procedures: 'The account books are a business diary that controls all commercial transactions and that quickly becomes a form of continuous self-control – it is not by chance that accounting has been seen as one of the origins of the modern diary. Every day becomes a day of balance and judgment, examined according to its returns.'[37]

Joseph Vogl describes bookkeeping as a practice that allows constant observation and monitoring of changing events. The bookkeeper manages events by recording them selectively in various books – daybook, journal and ledger – and sorting them into profit and loss. The events are recorded on the axis of time and within specific time units which apply across the board. Such a notation ensures continuity and an impression of endlessness.

For the merchant, the introduction of bookkeeping means that he becomes as it were sleepless, forever restless and vigilant, 'a subject of balance sheets, annual statements and continuous self-control; a subject who places a layer of account books between himself and worldly events'.[38] No unit of time must be wasted and no action unproductive, and since business success is identified with biographical success, the same recordable measures of success are applied to business and life alike.

A parallel economization process is also observable in the context of modern industrial labour. In premodern times, a craftsman would make a given item, say a cabinet, according to the needs and specifications of the customer. The work ended with the completion of the cabinet and was remunerated

directly on that basis – in other words, its purpose lay in the
final product. Industrial production, on the other hand, is
no longer concerned with the manufacture of an individual
product as an end in itself and labour as the means to that
end: it is a system of ceaseless activity aimed at generating
a theoretically infinite series of products in order to create
added value in the shape of investment capital, which is
then ploughed back immediately into improving production
or expanding the product range. In this way, all limits are
removed from production: nothing is ever finished; the work
never stops.

This model implies not only a reversal of means and end
– labour and money become the end, the products and their
manufacture merely the means – but also the theoretical
'interminability of activity' and a fundamental 'futility of production'.[39] Herein lies, as we can see, not only the root of the
notion of unlimited growth but also the modern basis for the
mentality of a never-finished, never-ending human being.

Accompanying this trend towards interminable activity
and never-ending growth are also changes in the perception
of time: not just in terms of industrial working time, which is
clocked and synchronized instead of individually determined,
but also the huge acceleration of movement through space in
the nineteenth century following the introduction of steam-
and later petrol-driven vehicles – what historian Wolfgang
Schivelbusch, in *The Railway Journey*, has described as the
'industrialization of time and space'.[40] This parallel industrialization of time and space perception has led to a continuously
escalating form of mobility whereby huge amounts of money
are considered worth investing in order to shave minutes off
journeys of hundreds of miles. This perceived 'time saving' goes
hand in hand with another often overlooked achievement of
the modern age in this respect: the spectacular increase in life
expectancy mentioned earlier. Only with increased life expectancy can such as a thing as a personal future be imagined, and

with it the possibility of making a life plan – something we now take for granted.

At the same time, the ever-increasing lifespan made possible not just by the welfare state but also by medical progress supports the notion that, like the economy, it too is in a process of continuous growth. What's more, economic man, who is free to make individual life choices and must get the most out of his time on earth, no longer sees himself as existing within a supratemporal generational context in which his own lifespan is merely one episode in a consecutive and interlinked series of lives: from now on, he is focused entirely on his own life.[41] All the more reason, then, to maximize the time available by saving, using and accumulating as much of it as possible.

The same trend also has a further implication: there is a new emphasis on the category of energy, particularly once fossil fuels come into play. The switch from biomass to coal and oil in industrially advanced countries such as Britain, France and Germany not only created a fateful disparity between the West and all other countries of the world,[42] but also led to a sudden popularization of the notion of energetic activity, something not found in other parts of the world:

> The energy-rich and self-consciously 'energetic' West presented itself accordingly to the rest of the world. The cultural heroes of the age were not contemplative idlers, religious ascetics, or tranquil scholars but practitioners of the *vita activa*: indefatigable conquerors, intrepid travellers, restless researchers, imperious captains of industry. Wherever they appeared on the scene, Westerners impressed, terrified, or bluffed people with a personal dynamism that was supposed to represent their society of origin.[43]

Also associated with this is, of course, the (white) western sense of superiority, whose far-reaching consequences are still

felt today, as the simultaneously emerging racial theory clas-
sified 'races' not just according to physical characteristics but
also in terms of their alleged productivity and energy.

The emerging discipline of psychology, too, is peppered with
the energy concepts of the industrial age. It is an almost forgotten fact nowadays that one of nineteenth-century psychology's
historic achievements was the ability to measure nerve activity
following the discovery that it was based on electrical energy.
In 1849, the physiologist Hermann von Helmholtz had successfully demonstrated that electrical impulses took a certain time
to travel along the nerve fibres. Early experimental psychology
focused on the measurement of stimulus intensity in relation
to energy input, while the emerging field of psychophysics
made major contributions to the optimization of human–
machine interaction. But it would be quite wrong to attribute
the notion of mind energy to the scientific side of psychology
alone; the works of Sigmund Freud too, for example, abound
with references to the mechanics, hydraulics and energetics
of the industrial age. The concept of (free and bound) 'energy'
plays as important a role in psychoanalysis as the 'drive' and
its 'dynamic'. Other prominent concepts are 'displacement',
'stasis', 'compression' and, interestingly, the 'economics' of our
inner life. Even in the famous *Language of Psychoanalysis*, we
still find examples of engineer-speak such as 'mental processes
consist in the circulation and distribution of a measurable
energy (drive energy) that can be increased or reduced and can
be equivalent to other forms of energy'.[44]

In other words, the workings of the psyche were likened in
the imagination to those of a steam engine. As such, it is no
wonder that the emerging discipline of educational science was
principally aimed at subduing and controlling sexual energies,
as the science historian Michael Hagner has demonstrated.[45]

The invention of school as an institution for educating all
members of a society is another aspect of the development
of industrially advanced countries, whereby the emphasis

was as much on its disciplinary function as on the transfer of knowledge. The school regime served to inculcate the kind of virtues – punctuality, cleanliness, diligence, order, etc. – that an industrial system needs. After all, the division of labour can only function if working time is synchronized, i.e., if workers perform their tasks simultaneously and according to a precisely timed cycle. Our social character is shaped by the need for synchronization in a highly specialized industrial society. Drilling competitiveness and measuring individual performance via grading systems are part of that mindset. This schooling process persists to this day: not only are enrolment rates and literacy levels still regarded as key markers of 'development',[46] but the micromanagement of all aspects of learning and education based on *measurable* performance criteria also remains the norm. Today's school and university students struggle to imagine an education or career that has no direct purpose or commercial function and exists outside the realm of competition and certificates of achievement. The concept of learning is understood solely as the accumulation, appropriation and storage of 'more' knowledge and endless information.

The enduring impact of such thought patterns, which I call 'mental infrastructures',[47] was illustrated during the COVID crisis when a grotesquely inadequate set of education ministers insisted stubbornly and against all medical reason on the importance of pressing ahead with face-to-face tuition – as if Germany were still in the Wilhelmine era. At all events, this brief historical reconstruction goes to show how the notions of energy, diligence, discipline, performance measurement and, notably, the boundless escalation of all things came to be part of the social character of modern man. And is no doubt also deeply ingrained in anyone reading this book.

Unlimited enlightenment

There is a crack in everything,
that's how the light gets in.
                    Leonard Cohen

'Enlightenment, understood in the widest sense as the advance
of thought, has always aimed at liberating human beings from
fear and installing them as masters. Yet the wholly enlightened
earth is radiant with triumphant calamity. Enlightenment's
program was the disenchantment of the world.'[48] Thus begins
the main text of Max Horkheimer and Theodor W. Adorno's
famous book *Dialectic of Enlightenment*. Or not so much a
book as a sequence of fragments: by 1944, the authors had
abandoned the attempt to make it the definitive work on the
critical theory of contemporary society that they had envisaged
while in exile in the United States. This collection is unfinished,
its parts don't even fit together, and yet it is considered one of
the most important works in the history of philosophy. Why?
Precisely *because* of its unfinished, fragmentary nature.

As Umberto Eco observed in his wonderful book *Lector in
Fabula*, reading is always a process of active textual cooperation: the reader fills in those elements that the author leaves
out in order to prevent the narrative from becoming endless,
boring or redundant. When we read 'He boarded the bus',
for example, we don't need telling that a bus is a means of
transport. We bring this knowledge implicitly to the text: that's
how it works. We can imagine for ourselves what sort of coat
the protagonist is wearing or how cold a medieval castle is
in winter, and we are constantly adding these details to the
text as we go. Thus the reader is part, and co-producer, of the
text – not a reader *of*, but a reader *in* the story: *lector in fabula*.
It is the gaps in the text, then, that are filled by the active,
cooperative, participatory activity of reading, and it is this that
constitutes knowledge.

In the same way, the gaps in the *Dialectic of Enlightenment* generate a cognitive process. The individual fragments are not all equally good but, strangely enough, the fragmentary nature of the work means that certain parts, once read, remain indelibly printed on the mind. As does their clear articulation of a point which modernity is increasingly inclined to dodge the more it advances.

'Enlightenment is totalitarian.' This statement appears on page four: a relatively abrupt and simple one amid a string of complex and difficult compound sentences. Yet it was this sentence in particular that I struggled with for a long time. Hang on, I thought, enlightenment is the basis of my autonomy and freedom: how can it be totalitarian? Totalitarianism refers to hermetically sealed, closed systems, constructs or states that refuse to let in any outside influences and don't need ideas, just obedient learners. What could possibly be totalitarian about enlightenment?

The answer according to Horkheimer and Adorno is this:

> Human beings purchase the increase in their power with estrangement from that over which it is exerted. Enlightenment stands in the same relation to things as the dictator to human beings. He knows them to the extent that he can manipulate them. The man of science knows things to the extent that he can make them. Their 'in-itself' becomes 'for him'.[49]

This is a very apt description of our relationship with nature. The world is one big arsenal of tools for achieving certain goals, not a thing 'in itself' but one that is *'for* something' – a storehouse of matter, in the terminology of Francis Bacon, one of the founders of our modern understanding of science. The totalitarian aspect of enlightenment lies in the legitimation of this relationship with nature which not only sees every animal, plant or stone as having no value of its own, only a value 'for me', but also ignores the fact that we too are part of nature.

I don't mean this in any esoteric sense; as biological organisms, our ontological status is no higher than that of any other animal. We are born with a genetic disposition that develops in a particular way according to our environment; our existence depends on the reliable operation of our metabolism and a fixed body temperature; we reproduce; and eventually we die, whether from organ failure, disease or an act of violence.

In this respect, as fellow animals, we *are* nature, and enlightenment has allowed us to make these huge advances precisely because of our ability to systematically ignore that fact. Or to put it another way: it was the ability to systematically disregard our animal nature that allowed us to view the natural world as something apart from ourselves, something that stands in various relations to us: benign, hostile, conquerable, exploitable and so on. As Eva von Redecker writes, 'Perhaps our basic mistake is seeing nature as a backdrop. As if an immovable stage had been built for us humans, as if we weren't made of the same stuff.'[50]

A group selfie with nature as a backdrop: that's the best way to imagine the mindset that allowed us to make such incredible advances in terms of controlling and exploiting nature, leading to those great strides in life expectancy, health, wealth, freedom and world share of which rich societies are the chief beneficiaries. Modernity is a socio-technical figuration that has transformed the world. And, with it, our understanding of the nature of development, progress, growth, education and so on. The concept of endlessness coupled with continuous growth only became possible with the apparent liberation of economics from the biological limits of value creation.

Which brings us back to our central point that all the achievements of modern civilization are built on the boundless exploitation of natural resources. The German Left has always dwelt exclusively on one half of Marx's theory, and the Greens on the other:

All progress in capitalistic agriculture is a progress in the art, not only of robbing the labourer, but of robbing the soil; all progress in increasing the fertility of the soil for a given time, is a progress towards ruining the lasting sources of that fertility. The more a country starts its development on the foundations of modern industry . . . the more rapid is this process of destruction. Capitalist production, therefore, develops technology . . . only by sapping the original sources of all wealth – the soil and the worker.[51]

Take the example of Giga Berlin, the huge Tesla factory recently opened – with the aid of billions of euros of taxpayers' money and at the expense of a large area of forest – by the billionaire digital tech giant Elon Musk. This anachronistic project was supported by the city council and state administration, both of which have Greens and Social Democrats in their number. Yet in it every conceivable abstraction from the wellsprings of Elon Musk's wealth converge as if under a magnifying glass. It is utter madness that such an ecologically, politically and economically outdated giga project, and one that sends out entirely the wrong signal, should be greeted with such euphoria after half a century of environmental campaigning. Where Karl Marx once cited three sources of value creation – capital, labour *and* nature – all that remains today is the frankly idiotic focus on 'expected returns'. One person sees electric cars as progressive, another jobs, but, astonishingly, the fact that such a project is destructive on every front doesn't seem to bother anyone. The conservationists do their bit to resettle the slow worm, and everyone's happy.

Reflecting on such examples, one can't help but agree with the philosopher Bruno Latour: no, we have never been modern. We already forfeited that possibility when we separated 'nature' and 'man' and set them up as opposites, so that all forms of limitation were simply airbrushed out of the picture. Labour is an inexhaustible commodity as long as there

Fig. 1.11:   Tesla Gigafactory: the twenty-first century is
unimaginable without the motor car

are human beings; nature is not. Hence the mess in which the
success story of modernity now finds itself.

In the twentieth century alone, the global economy grew
fourfold, energy consumption sixteenfold and production
fortyfold. More energy was consumed in those hundred
years than in the preceding two hundred millennia of human
history – and ten times as much as in the millennium before
the twentieth century. And most of it was accounted for by
Europe and North America. Meanwhile, the principle of the
growth-based economy has spread around the globe, and it is
an attractive one because it produces a visible and perceptible
improvement in people's living conditions within a short space
time. As the historian Dipesh Chakrabarty has pointed out,
the 'great acceleration' in rates of consumption and the deple-
tion of resources provoked by our modern relationship with
nature represents, for those societies which have undergone or

are still undergoing that process, a phase of emancipation and expansion of individual agency.

The historically unique success of the economic and social model that is now reaching its limits was *not just material*, however: it brought the populations of advanced industrial societies democracy, the rule of law and protection against bodily harm, together with prosperity, health, education and social welfare on an unprecedented scale. It is this very success that is luring the project of human civilization into a fatal trap, as it is becoming apparent, in the wake of climate change and species extinction (among many other issues), that the civilizing project of modernity was only able to function so spectacularly because of our consistent disregard of nature.

It's fair to say that, ever since the advent of growth-based capitalism, we have been engaged in an ongoing dispute with nature. But for 200 years, it was a one-sided one: only we did the talking. Only in the last half a century have we begun to get answers, and, the longer we refuse to listen to them, the louder and clearer they become.

Which brings us back to the dialectic of enlightenment: what Horkheimer and Adorno established is that the constantly improving technologies for controlling nature and ourselves that enlightenment has brought us have made it possible to ignore the fact that, first, nature cannot be controlled and, second, wherever this is attempted, it damages our subjectivity – the very thing that raises humans above the status of purely natural beings. 'There is no being in the world that knowledge cannot penetrate, but what can be penetrated by knowledge is not being.'[52] This is the modern drama in a nutshell: the project of total control over nature also eliminates the very identity and freedom of the individual that enlightenment was meant to fight for. Being can never be fully explained, just as nature can never be fully controlled. In this sense, enlightenment actually reverts to the thing it sought to replace: mythology.

'Human beings have always had to choose between their subjugation to nature and its subjugation to the self.'[53] This statement highlights an irresolvable conflict of the human condition – and because it is irresolvable, we have no choice but to recognize it. We cannot think and act contrarily to the reality that humans are natural beings and that all the achievements of modern civilization are based on the fiction of endlessness which, conversely, *must* ignore the natural basis of life if it is to be maintained. The day when dead mass overtakes living mass will, as it were, be the day when the dialectic of enlightenment departs from the arcane (or, in modern parlance, non-system relevant) realm of philosophy and becomes a tangible reality. This totalitarian and mythicized enlightenment devours everything in its path.

What we need is a new and different enlightenment fit for the twenty-first century – one that recognizes the limits of our control over nature and the self and cultivates a new relationship with nature.

You can't bargain with nature

If it was a mistake to regard nature as the backdrop for the universal selfie of *Homo sapiens*, it is equally illusory to think that we can still, by dint of ever-improving technology, conquer a natural world that is telling us on a daily basis, in the shape of climate change and species loss, that it can't be done. The COVID pandemic has taught us the important lesson that you can't negotiate or do deals with a virus. And the same goes for all the things on which human life depends: thermoregulation and an intact biosphere are non-negotiable criteria.

Consequently, all efforts to thrash out international climate treaties – whose implementation is then subject to further national negotiations aimed at reconciling economic, political and social interests with the ecological imperative – are irrational and, in a way, childish. Since there is no choice but to negotiate with stakeholders from the world of business, politics and trade unions, the outcome is, paradoxically, a bargain with nature. OK, climate, here's the deal: we've calculated that you can absorb another 580 gigatons of CO_2 by 2050, so kindly do so. In return, we promise to stop emitting CO_2 and 'decarbonize' our continuously growing economy. Shake on it?

Clearly, such a climate policy is plain anthropomorphism dressed up as politics. Kids' stuff. After half a century of environmental campaigning, it's time to grow up, forget the idea of trying to do a deal and take on board the feedback we are constantly receiving from the earth and climate system. The fiction of endless progress based on endless business as usual needs to be dispelled by a culture capable of learning the art of stopping. Growing up is the process by which you learn that you can't have everything you once thought you could.

After my heart attack, my perspective changed, and I saw my own little world through new eyes. I don't wish to romanticize, but since then my values have shifted; the world is still the same, but I see it differently. And that's the point. Losing my illusion of mortality isn't a cause for sadness but a new beginning. From now on, I can tell a new story about myself. Which is also, incidentally, the basis of any successful psychoanalysis: patients learn to tell a new story about themselves because they have learnt to see themselves from a different angle. Adopting a new perspective or using a new conceptual or descriptive system is crucial because it allows us to see the same reality in a different light and hence to access it in different ways.

Earlier on, I quoted Wittgenstein's dictum that the solution to the riddle of life in time and space lies outside time and space. Only when we accept that there is a residue of human existence that cannot be explained can we shed the hubristic notion of complete power over nature and begin to see the world differently. I have always been fascinated by the

image Wittgenstein develops for describing the world in his
Tractatus Logico-philosophicus:

> Let us imagine a white surface with irregular black spots. We
> now say: Whatever kind of picture these make I can always
> get as near as I like to its description, if I cover the surface
> with a sufficiently fine square network and now say of every
> square that it is white or black. In this way I shall have brought
> the description of the surface to a unified form. This form is
> arbitrary, because I could have applied with equal success a
> net with a triangular or hexagonal mesh. It can happen that
> the description would have been simpler with the aid of a
> triangular mesh; that is to say, we might have described the
> surface more accurately with a triangular, and coarser, than
> with the finer square mesh, or vice versa, and so on. To the
> different networks correspond different systems of describing
> the world.[54]

The premise that there are *different* systems of describing
the world is a far cry from the premise that everything could
in theory be fully described within a single system, but that we
have, alas, 'not yet' reached that point. Paradoxically, by grimly
pursuing the notion of boundlessness, this assumption actually limits the range of human possibilities. Conversely – and
equally paradoxically – we must learn to expand that range by
viewing our limits as a starting point.

The realm of possibility lies within, not outside, us.

The heart

It's amazing what emotions the sight of your own heart arouses
when you undergo a catheterization procedure or ultrasound
scan, for example. The way it beats. What an incredibly intricate
organ it is that sees us through our entire lifecycle from start to

finish. Even more astonishing is the fact that it starts beating in the foetus from the twenty-second day of pregnancy; from then on, it goes on pumping with stoical regularity and strength for a hundred years – if you're very lucky. As the centre of vitality, the heart has been steeped in myth for as long as we have evidence of human existence; in contrast to the brain, it has always embodied the ego, the life force within us, the emotions that govern our life and, often enough, make it difficult. When the founder of the children's rights charity Terre des Hommes, Lutz Beisel – a man I greatly admire – was recovering from a heart attack and I asked him what had caused it, he replied 'Well, Mr Welzer, I do take things so much to heart.'

Such expressions – to take something to heart, to have a big heart, to take heart – are far more than just metaphors. The still young discipline of psycho-cardiology studies the inter-relationships between psychological pressures such as grief, stress and critical life events on one hand and cardiovascular disease on the other. There are phenomena, such as 'broken heart syndrome', whose symptoms can resemble those of a heart attack, but which can be triggered by a highly stressful event such as lovesickness, for example. It is this fascinating connection between body and (if you like) spirit that causes the heart to be assigned such an important role in our culture, from popular lore to songs, iconography and literature. People carve hearts into the bark of trees and wear gingerbread hearts round their neck at Oktoberfests.

You can 'wear your heart on your sleeve', 'pour your heart out' to someone, 'break someone's heart', talk about a matter 'close to your heart', 'lose your heart' to someone, be either 'soft-' or 'hard-hearted' and so on and so forth – and the meaning is instantly clear in each case.

While the brain has been known for a few thousand years to be the seat of consciousness and director of all bodily functions – including the pumping action of the heart – we somehow feel a closer connection to the heart. We don't just know but

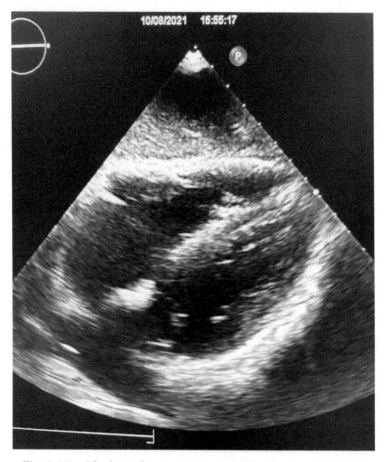

Fig. 1.12:   The heart beats approx. 2.7 billion times in a lifetime

feel it to be the vital centre of our system, and as such it is perhaps also the organ that reminds us most forcefully that we are natural beings, biological bodies. Hence the remarkable moment of insight you get when you actually see your own heart beating. You suddenly realize that we are not first and foremost brainworkers, intellectuals or even thinkers, but organisms whose basic function is regulated and guaranteed via this wondrous, intricate, delicate muscle. Listen to your heartbeat, as the song goes.

The best strophes are catastrophes

The title of this chapter is borrowed from the media theorist Peter Weibel, formerly an artist and punk musician with
the Austrian band Hotel Morphila Orchester. And it's true:
catastrophes – as long as they don't affect us – do inspire a
certain thrill, a mixture of pleasure and fear. There is something strangely intriguing about them, perhaps because of the
sense that they could occur at any time – which is why we
are glad when they happen elsewhere and to other people.
A special category is that of the ultimate catastrophe or
Apocalypse – the end of everything and everyone. Since the
Age of Enlightenment, the Apocalypse, too, has become secularized as a human-induced phenomenon. In earlier times,
it was perceived as an ever-present threat of punishment for
fallen man's failure to lead a god-fearing or godly lifestyle. At
the height of the era of cultural pessimism, it was cast as the
downfall, if not of the world, then at least of the West. Later,
the danger was perceived as lying in political constellations
which, during the Cold War 'balance of terror' of the nuclear
powers, held the potential to annihilate the entire human race
many times over (and still do, although no one seems to care
any more). And nowadays, it is located in scientific scenarios
of a climate apocalypse threatening to engulf us if emission
targets are not reached.

Personally, I find the notion of the Apocalypse a very comforting one: after all, the most upsetting thing about your own
death is the fact that everyone else will still be around when
you've gone. If we all have to die at the same time, no one has
to miss out on any parties they might have gone to if they were
still alive. No more FOMO. That seems a pretty good deal to
me and, should the Apocalypse occur, I would embrace it.

But that's the only good thing to be said about the end
of the world. Because, unlike the apocalypses of premodern
times, the modern variety don't offer the possibility of a benign

afterworld. An apocalypse may be the end of everything human related, but it is by no means the only kind of end. In a lecture, the philosopher Ludger Heidbrink enumerated the many and varied possible forms which the end of civilization could take:

> The end comes in the form of apocalypse, catastrophe, ruin and bankruptcy; as downfall, collapse and erosion. The end manifests itself in crisis, decision and upheaval, in revolution, *coup d'état* and liberation. We experience the end when taking our leave, parting, splitting up. We reach the end when we arrive at a destination, complete a task, implement a programme, conclude a process, meet a quota, draw up a balance sheet. The end can be the drying up of funds, the depletion of resources, the consumption of materials. We encounter the end in terms of shortage, stagnation, an expired deadline, a limit reached. As these examples show, the semantic spectrum of finality is itself virtually endless.[55]

If there are so many different ends, why do we have no concept of finitude? Why do we live our lives and do business as if things went on for ever? Perhaps for that very reason. Perhaps all our evocations of possible end scenarios, whether comforting or frightening, enable us to ignore the actual fact of finitude itself, to talk and act as if it didn't exist. We behave as if we were merely observers of finitude and distract ourselves with all manner of doomsday fantasies. This has the psychological advantage of allowing us to cultivate entirely false visions of the end and all possible ends – as if ending were a sudden, abrupt event, bringing everything to a close in an instant. The buzzword in this context is 'disruptive': fans of this concept rave about the 'creative destruction' of old business models, thereby overlooking the fact that, by contributing to rising consumption, they are guilty of a highly uncreative and indeed wholly destructive form of destruction. The impact of this is not instantaneous, nor does it hit everyone: climate change for example affects different groups in very different ways, from the population of an archipelago like the Maldives, at risk of being swallowed up by rising sea levels, to nomadic herders losing their pastureland to persistent droughts, to people in rich economies squeezing in a last flight to the Maldives before they disappear, yet fretting about the rise in forest fires. In other words, while in some parts of the world climate change is a topic of conversation at parties, it is already a cause of death in others. There is no such thing as 'the Apocalypse': it is made up of a series of temporally and geographically diverse events whose consequences, depending on the level of impact, are death, forced migration, a thrill of excitement or just plain indifference.

This compensatory function of doomsday scenarios is also highlighted by the literary scholar Eva Horn, who refers to the

> imagined catastrophe as an excuse for inaction. We consume disaster scenarios and disaster science, but we do it largely from our viewpoint as spectators. In other words, we experience destruction vicariously. Because disasters are something that happens to others – sometimes brave screen heroes or poor college professors, sometimes faceless victims such as those living near nuclear reactors, remote island peoples or landscapes. . . . But this 'experience' takes place in a space that we keep strictly separate from the space in which we live, take decisions and make plans. In this future, it's always someone else who perishes – even though I know that what I'm witnessing could be my future too.[56]

It is this attitude that the author and journalist Roger Willemsen intended to make the subject of a book he never got to write. In a lecture, he outlined some of his thoughts in the future perfect mode, i.e., that of an anticipated past:

> We were like the countryside – retreating. We could do nothing to resist our own disappearance, yet we wore ourselves

down within the narrow confines of a job that was supposed
to make a company stronger, more successful and more effective, but that would not answer any existential questions or
help to guarantee our survival. Looking into the past, we spied
only progress. Looking into the future, we saw nothing but
decadence.[57]

For the lucky ones in this staggered, drawn-out catastrophe, there is no need to resist our disappearance; for now, it's
others who are disappearing. Hence the fact that no attention is paid to questions of survival: other things appear much
more important. And by this omission, we place ourselves in
a no man's land between past and future – an ever-expanding,
seemingly timeless present. We behave as if we were merely
spectators of past and future events: 'We were those who knew
but did not understand, who grasped but could not imagine,
filled with information but devoid of insight, crammed with
knowledge but scant of experience. So we went, no longer
detained by ourselves.'[58]

Ever onwards. What we are busy beavering away at is the
magic project of 'creating a world outside the conditions of its
own existence'. As I remarked earlier, the space for change lies
inside, not outside, our own limits, and the time for change is
the present, not the past or future. That space and that time are
all we have, and even if the progress model of modernity, now
degraded to a fetish of never-ending, 'away-from-here' innovation, does spur us on to an imagined step beyond the limits of
the here and now, it is of little use when the feedback from our
relationship with nature is telling us: sorry, folks, it was good
while it lasted, but it's over now.

The time for externalizing the costs of our lifestyle to other
times and other spaces is past: the problems have grown too
pressing for that. There is no viewing platform from which
we can observe doomsday scenarios and collapses with a bit-
tersweet thrill: it is time for reality. Right now. According

to Roger Willemsen, we are facing a new imperative, 'which demands that we be present – not on remote displays, not in the modules of our outsourced intelligence, not in the digital parallel world of the social that is superimposed on the reality of this social asociality, but in the practical world where we are once again facing the question of our collective survival'.[59]

The twenty-first century is already old, yet we still think of it as young

At the time of writing, it is 2021. More than a fifth of the century is already over. And that fifth of a century has seen no sign of a change in our direction of travel, even though global problems have been coming thicker and faster than in the latter part of the twentieth century. The United States and Europe have wasted time and energy on a completely senseless 'war on terror', sacrificed state welfare provision for the sake of neoliberal propaganda and made businesses more vulnerable, unleashed an obscene financial industry and failed to rein it in again despite the global economic crisis it has caused. Europe allows refugees to drown and makes pacts with autocrats and militias. Around the globe, we have invited dangerous clowns into the political arena; in Europe, we have failed to develop even the germ of a modern migration policy; and, in Germany, we have no party capable of seeing environmental and social problems as two sides of the same coin. At the same time, everyone admires the havoc wreaked by squillionaires from the digital tech industry and does nothing to stop their surveillance and colonization of our lifeworld. Although all this has been moving in the same direction for two decades now, we somehow seem to believe we are still in the twentieth century. When almost everything was even better. I nearly wrote: when there was still hope.

During this time, the chances of those born in the interim being able to shape their own future without being severely limited by the increasingly precarious climatic conditions, the growing proportion of dead mass, the emptying of the oceans and forests and our predilection for filling spaces with stuff, have fallen significantly by comparison with my generation of baby boomers. Intergenerational justice is an ethical criterion of the second millennium: it no longer applies in the third. The future is prematurely exhausted; as the literary theorist Albrecht Koschorke has noted, the more contested and denuded the space has become, the more the exploitation of resources has shifted into the dimension of time. Competition between the established older generation and younger outsiders has become more overt – the old no longer make any bones about their lack of interest in a future beyond their own lifetime. Particularly in societies where the age structure is systematically skewed in favour of the elderly, they are a far more electorally relevant target group for political parties than the young.

The same pattern is reflected systemically in the management of the COVID crisis. What have things come to when a – by global standards – super-rich society finds itself utterly incapable of organizing a school system that promotes meaningful learning, healthy social mixing, self-organization and initiative by means of digital technology, the abolition of the year-group principle, the abandonment of grades and much else besides that could have been learnt from decades of experience on the part of schools with successful alternative and international models? Instead, an intellectually ossified or else corrupt bunch of education ministers could come up with nothing better than cramming young people into classrooms in winter at a time of high infection rates and opening the windows every twenty minutes, like something from the dark days of the Wilhemine era. Although at least the education policy of that time was ideologically motivated. These irresponsible men and women, almost all of them devoid of any pedagogical training, and all

of them non-immigrant-background German, were respond-
ing solely to commercial interests keen to avoid too many lost
working hours due to home schooling. You could hardly treat
an up-and-coming generation with more contempt.

Or look at the way the well-founded demands of the Fridays
for Future movement have been brushed aside by a federal government that, instead of making decisive plans for the future, is
stuck in the past and keeps obsolete industries artificially alive
so that they can go on destroying the planet. Please excuse
the rant, but I do at least have the German Constitutional
Court on my side since its ruling at the end of April 2020
that the freedom of future generations should be protected.
That said, when you consider the disregard in which the young
generation are currently held, you cannot but wonder who
will fight for democracy, for a European Union, and for the
values it seeks daily to uphold, only to be trampled underfoot.
A new generation that is treated with such condescension and
contempt? One that is expected to bear without question the
consequences of a knowingly wrong policy?

A few years ago, the sociologist Stephan Lessenich wrote a
book about the 'externalization society': ever since the days of
imperialism, rich societies have plundered the globe for raw
materials, turning them into ever more products with ever
shorter lifetimes and product cycles and then exporting the
waste to countries where no one could ever have afforded the
products that rich countries simply throw away after use (and
sometimes even before). This spatial externalization has its
temporal counterpart in the intergenerational relationship:
here, the commodity being consumed is not space but life
years – those of the next generation. And it is this aspect in
particular that comes across in the depressing exchanges we
see time and time again on television between representatives
of the 'concrete generation' and young political activists. It
would be almost refreshing if someone from the concrete fac-
tion were to say: 'Dear Ms Thunberg, I am not interested in

Fig. 1.13:   TV panel discussion: talking to concrete

what you have to say. I expect to live another 20 years, and I
want everything to stay as it is. You are cramping my style.'
Instead, we get the same old line that the powers that be are
aware of the problem and are doing everything within their –
naturally limited – means. Blah blah blah. And the attempt to
bargain with the climate system continues.

Let's face it: the fact that the current generation of so-called
economic and political decision makers can afford the luxury
of acting as if the climate system – indeed, the earth system
itself – could be negotiated with depends upon the exploitation of their own children's future. Because if we plot the
problems of the twenty-first century along the axes of time
and generativity, things look very different. The consequences
of decisions taken in 2021 – such as the commissioning of new
coal power stations – will be felt in 2051. By then, the 'decision makers' will be dead, leaving the living to deal with the
problem. This is organized irresponsibility. The as yet unborn
cannot employ lobbyists.

A relationship with nature that was founded and built on
externalization and, as such, has insisted both theoretically and
practically on a strict differentiation between 'man and nature'

has surely had its day when, on top of the increasingly negative feedback from the climate system and biosphere, the whole principle of generativity is abandoned. While ultra-progressive queer couples in affluent countries hire surrogate mothers in India or Ukraine to conceive and carry their designer babies – mothers who receive a pittance in return for the exploitation of their bodies and never see their children again – infant mortality in less fortunate parts of the world is still almost one in ten. And this will only get worse as the habitable spaces of the earth continue to shrink. In short, we are witnessing an empirical trend whose continuation is not only incompatible with a civilized society but also represents a radical limitation of future human potential. Because that potential depends on the principle of natality.

What does it mean to be born human?

The human condition is both profoundly social and co-evolutionary – two aspects that are closely intertwined. Our modern self-image as human beings, shaped as it is by the twin influences of philosophy and conventional economics, can scarcely be described as reflective of that condition. The sociologist Norbert Elias once said to the philosopher Iring Fetscher in a television debate: 'You see, philosophers always think of humans as adults who were never children.' Fetscher was somewhat taken aback by this, and no wonder: with this insightful remark, Elias had just swept away the whole concept of alterity – the branch of philosophy that studies the mutual relationship of ego and alter ego and how they interact and negotiate with each other. This question is a misleading one because humans have always been part of relationships. We are always 'we' before we become 'I'.

After all, long before our reflexive self-consciousness awakens at the age of three or four and we learn to say 'I', we will have already been constantly in the company of others – parents, siblings and other key figures. And that togetherness will have given us a practical familiarity with countless everyday concepts and their meanings. We will have experienced them through the practice of socialization: not 'learned' or 'internalized' them, but actually lived them. Since both the organic maturation of the brain and the generation of new nerve cells and the establishment of their network structures continue for a long time after birth and in some cases over a whole lifetime, we can say that the human brain develops, forms and structures itself based on social experience. In other words, the development of the brain is experience dependent and defined by interaction with others.

Neurons change in response to external stimuli, and so, inevitably, do the networks with which they are associated. The neuronal representations of individual elements of our experience of the outside world become more stable the more frequently they are activated. These patterns arise – increasingly over the course of our development – from the interaction between the child's genetically predisposed biochemical and neurophysiological development processes and the signals and information that come from its environment and particularly its micro-environment. A substantial part of this – since the child naturally grows up within a social context – consists of interpersonal exchange and, later on, intersubjective experience. It was this fact that led the psychiatrist Daniel Siegel to coin the phrase 'human connections form neuronal connections', and prompted the anthropologist Bradd Shore to publish his impressive book *Culture in Mind* (1996).[60]

A child is born with a range of active perceptual and differentiational skills. Developmental psychology offers a wealth of evidence that a newborn already actively engages with the people around it and comes ready equipped with a number of capabilities that allow it to appropriate the world. Of course, its developmental genes provide a whole set of basic circuits that have nothing to do with experience but are, as it were, hardwired for survival purposes. These include the basic abilities that used to be called 'unconditional reflexes' – the grip reflex that makes a newborn grasp a proffered finger, the sucking reflex and so on. The fact that the baby can breathe, see, hear, feel, ingest food, feel pain – all this is not the result of experience but of genetic determination, as in other animals too.

Also built into the universe of these basic circuits, however, is the potential for new ones to form that are *not* preprogrammed but subject to experience. 'The genetically determined circuits already predispose the developing brain towards very specific sensory perceptions, a specific associative processing of those impressions, and the activation of very specific behavioural and (emotional) responses.'[61] This potential for associative perception, storage and recall is partly the result of a uniquely human genetic disposition, but it is also the thing that allows human development processes to easily override genetic preprogramming. A large part of the connecting architecture of the human brain is developed through experience – a certain sequence of sounds, for example, will form a specific engram, or memory trace, in the brain. The potential for this engram to be formed, and how, is genetically determined, but not the form of the engram itself, which depends, for instance, on the sound structure of the mother's voice. Michael Tomasello calls this 'transactional causality': 'maturational capacities create the possibility of new kinds of experiences and learning, and then those learning experiences are the proximate causes of development.'[62]

A baby – like any other living creature – is born with a genetic predisposition for its neuronal architecture to develop and form connections, but the form that architecture takes depends on the cultural practice into which it is born. In humans, the brain of a newborn only weighs around a quarter of that of an adult. In chimpanzees – our nearest genetic relative – it weighs a good 60 per cent of the adult brain. Humans are the only species in which the number of neuronal circuits continues to grow after birth at the same rate and scale as in the foetus. Roughly 30,000 synapses occur every second below every square centimetre of the brain's surface – right up until the age of six or thereabouts. And that's by no means the end of it. Some areas and organs of the brain only become fully mature at puberty (such as the frontal lobe); others (such as the temporal lobes) not until the end of adolescence.[63] In short: the human brain is an organ that remains remarkably unfinished for a remarkably long time.

The fact that humans are born organically 'premature', that is, without fully formed organs, means that, in human development, genetically programmed maturation processes coincide with social development processes: organic and social development occur *in parallel*. Nature and culture are co-evolutionary: they operate as a unit. And the development of the human brain is precisely geared to this arrangement. No other living creature exhibits such a high level of neuroplasticity, no brain is as unfinished as that of a human, none has such a high potential for adaptation to different and changing environmental conditions.

In summary, the brain is an incredibly experience-dependent organ. While our neuronal network as adults is subject to constant changes as we process information from within and outside the body, signals from the environment already trigger modifications in the developing neuronal systems of babies, infants and adolescents, and they continue to do so into adulthood. This means that they act directly on the brain's developing organizational structure and hence on the abilities of the developing personality to solve problems and appropriate the world. Humans are social beings both in terms of their cultural and cerebro-organic development. In short, humans do not exist in the singular. And our neuronal systems always develop within the context of a culture.

Natural culture

This is what makes the human condition so unique: culture and nature are co-evolutionary components of the same individual development process. And this is what makes possible the ratchet effect I talked about earlier with reference to Michael Tomasello's studies. This background, I believe, helps us to understand how the level of civilization of a particular culture always feeds into the developmental environment of every child born into it, and is thus embedded in a very deep sense in its biopsychosocial development. According to Michael Tomasello, 'The most basic cognitive and social processes that can be observed in developing children today all have evolutionary histories.'[64] To use the anthropologist Bradd Shore's term, we have a cultured brain, and this in itself means that distinctions between 'man and nature' or 'culture and nature' are misguided.

This becomes even clearer if we switch from the individual or ontogenetic level to the phylogenetic level – that of human evolutionary history. As we know, we share almost 99 per cent of our genetic sequences (98.8 per cent to be exact) with chimpanzees, yet they appear, both as individuals and in the manner of their coexistence, to exhibit only a very distant relationship with the human condition. While they are intelligent tool users who compete (sometimes quite ingeniously) for advantages and are even capable of deception and concealment, they do not cooperate in any systematic way and, notably, once they have developed a particular technique or form of communication, it remains limited to the relevant group and is not passed on by 'cultural' means. The ratchet – to retain Tomasello's image – doesn't click into place but keeps slipping back to the starting point. Each new generation starts from the same place as the previous one.

Although humans and chimpanzees have common ancestors, our evolutionary paths diverged six to eight million years ago, and it is notable that 'culture' also plays a decisive role in our different subsequent trajectories: as the anthropologist Carel van Schaik and biomathematician Karin Isler write,

> at the behavioural level, we differ [i.e., from non-human primates, HW] in terms of ecology, cognition, culture, life course, social organization and sexuality. We hunt and gather in a group, look after each other, have developed a unique intelligence closely connected with the use of language, and we actively pass on our skills and knowledge. Through culture, we have created complex artefacts, symbols and institutions. . . . In all life situations, we show a strong willingness to cooperate, not just with relatives, but also with non-relatives or strangers.[65]

Even in terms of the organization of life, culture is the distinguishing feature of the human condition. Summing up the impact of the ecological conditions in which *Homo sapiens*' ancestors had to secure their survival, the paleobiologist Friedemann Schrenk writes:

> Under the pressure of the environmental changes at that time [i.e., the first tool-based cultures of 2.5 million years ago, HW], it was precisely the hominids' capacity for cultural behaviour that gave rise to the genus Homo. By comparison with the robust pre-humans, our ancestors displayed greater behavioural flexibility – a development that ultimately led to a larger and more efficient brain.[66]

It was biocultural phylogenesis that led to the unique evolutionary strategy of the cultured brain and hence, for good or ill, to the incredible adaptability of the human condition – a strategy that makes our genus not just robust, but robust enough to destroy or displace other life forms to an extent never before accomplished by any other species. Nor is there any other species in zoological history that has decimated the means of its own existence as thoroughly as *Homo sapiens*, whose sapience appears to leave something to be desired when it comes to sustainability.

> Cumulative cultural evolution is only possible because all individuals of a particular generation mostly learn the same thing from their elders, and so this is reliable and stable over time for all individuals – which sets the stage for any of them to potentially innovate. Obviously, when adults normatively expect children to learn, and they enforce these normative expectations, this creates precisely the kind of cultural ratchet that keeps cultural knowledge and practices stable over time until a novel innovation occurs.[67]

In with the new

There will always be novelty in the world, for as long as children, or new generations, are born into it. Hannah Arendt expressed her own thoughts on this subject in her book *The Human Condition*. For Arendt, the key human characteristic is the capacity to act, and to do so freely and revocably. That capacity naturally includes the possibility of doing something wrong – but one can be socially released from the consequences of one's errors through the forgiveness of others. Banal though this may sound, it is central for Arendt, for in her view forgiveness is the key to freedom: 'Without being forgiven, released from the consequences of what we have done, our capacity to act would, as it were, be confined to one single deed from which we could never recover; we would remain the victims of its consequences forever.'[68]

According to Arendt's theory, forgiveness is in turn linked to the ability which she sees as the central organizational principle of human affairs: we can only tolerate and deal with the indeterminacy of the future, the uncertainty of expectation, by making promises to each other – individually in the form of declarations or contracts, and socially and culturally through various conventions, from the fulfilment of obligations to the assumption of responsibility. As Arendt writes, 'the remedy for unpredictability, for the chaotic uncertainty of the future, is contained in the faculty to make and keep promises.'[69]

It is true that human societies, and in particular modern democracies, are based on trust, and that trust always depends on something remaining as reliable and stable in the future as it is in the present. Promising therefore also entails responsibility, and whenever a promise cannot be kept due to chance events, unforeseeable circumstances, errors and so on, the capacity to forgive ensures that trust in general can be preserved intact. To me, this is not just a plausible, logical, well-argued theory, but an *attractive* theory about the human condition, as it hinges on the fundamental mutuality between human beings.

In this sense, humans should never be thought of as singular beings but always as interdependent in their speech and actions and, in terms of the consequences of their actions, not fixed but flexible. Things can be undone; we can extricate ourselves from situations that have gone wrong. For Arendt, therefore, politics depends on the capacity to promise and the 'good will to counter the enormous risks of action by readiness to forgive and to be forgiven, to make promises and to keep them'.[70] Such a morality arises directly from human interaction, and it is also the precondition for renewal. Because the human condition is not, Arendt argues, characterized by the 'deathlessness of self-sufficient nature',[71] and hence neither by inevitability nor unavoidability, but by the possibility of freedom. The faculty of action interrupts all predispositions and automatisms and makes it possible to intervene in and halt ongoing processes.

> The life span of man running toward death would inevitably carry everything human to ruin and destruction if it were not

for the faculty of interrupting it and beginning something new, a faculty which is inherent in action like an ever-present reminder that men, though they must die, are not born in order to die but in order to begin.[72]

During this period of time between birth and death, humans – in contrast to other animals – are not slaves to a fixed course of predetermined events and processes but can take action and thus 'start something new'. For Arendt, this principle of starting anew is embodied in the concept of natality, the fact of 'being born': 'The miracle that saves the world, the realm of human affairs, from its normal, "natural" ruin is ultimately the fact of natality, in which the faculty of action is ontologically rooted.'[73] Each of us is a newcomer to the existing population, and therefore each of us can use our faculty of action to take things in a new direction.

Few passages in Hannah Arendt's work are as moving and exhilarating as these pages of the *Human Condition*. Here Arendt uses the actions of Jesus of Nazareth to exemplify the essentially philosophical categories of forgiving, promising and beginning: instead of citing a fellow philosopher in support of her argument, she cites a living embodiment of human potential. Accordingly, her theory of action ends with the remarkable sentence: 'It is this faith in and hope for the world that found perhaps its most glorious and most succinct expression in the few words with which the Gospels announced their "glad tidings": "A child has been born unto us."'[74]

The Christian religion, with the figure of the Saviour as a baby, is indeed a story of open-endedness and beginning, and in that sense it is not a religion of laws but of possibilities. Such, at least, is Hannah Arendt's interpretation – a person normally light years away from anything religious – and from this she then proceeds to develop the concept of natality. The faculty of beginning is the condition for the faculty of stopping, and just as birth and death delimit the scope of action for the human lifespan, so the faculties of both beginning and stopping are the condition for human freedom. In other words, we must safeguard the conditions for those faculties, not jeopardize them by constantly narrowing our scope of action due to the ecological consequences of choosing the wrong path. Continuing to pursue a false relationship with nature will lead to a loss of freedom.

What we need, therefore, is a cultural model in which the beauty of stopping is accorded the necessary weight in order for the project of civilization to continue. I say again: improving or indeed optimizing processes that are heading in the wrong direction only makes things worse. Stopping is imperative: it is a human cultural technique that we must re-learn. Only then can we achieve a new beginning.

Question

Why does the past, before we existed, hold less terror than the future, when we will no longer exist?

II

Narratives of Stopping – and of Life

Is there such a thing as experts in the art of stopping? There is certainly no shortage of experts in the art of continuation and optimization. Strange creatures – freaks, even – given the crystal-clear reality that we won't get through this century if we go on as we are. They are all like the drunkard in the joke who searches for his lost key under the streetlamp because it's too dark everywhere else.

In which professions is the life skill of stopping called for? I wondered; where is it necessary for survival? My first thought was mountaineering – so I called

Reinhold Messner

He wasn't surprised by my question. Indeed, he told me he had abandoned roughly a third of all his ventures and expeditions because they turned out to be too dangerous or impracticable. And in his 'job', the decision to stop is obviously taken in extremely life-threatening circumstances. Like the time when he and a fellow mountaineer set out to tackle the almost 4,000-metre-high south face of the Dhaulagiri.

We hadn't even got halfway when we were suddenly overtaken by fear and had to climb down again in a hurry, realizing we'd taken on too much, we couldn't do this. We had underestimated the size and steepness of the ascent – it was a mistake right from the start. We abandoned the expedition, clearly recognizing that we had been too ambitious this time. What we didn't want to do was to reach the edge of impossibility only to die in the process.

Fear is the signal to stop. When you are no longer in control of the situation – provided you are of sound mind – you stop. This is a hard thing to do psychologically, as we all know from our own experience of much tamer hikes: after all, we have invested a great deal of effort to reach the point of return. And in the case of expeditions, a large amount of money and resources, too. The same goes for people who invest in shares: the principle of loss aversion leads them to keep on investing rather than withdraw, thereby throwing good money after bad. The tendency, therefore, is to keep going long after we should have turned back. This can be fatal, making us throw good energy after bad. Pros like Reinhold Messner, by contrast, don't push on to the 'edge of impossibility', but listen to their fear: 'Your common sense tells you: this is too much – come on, let's get out of here.' Without discussion or negotiation. 'A few glances were enough to signal to each other that it was time to give it up as a bad job.'

According to Messner, who is undoubtedly the world's most experienced and successful mountaineer – partly thanks to the meticulousness of his planning – there is only so much you can predict:

After all, we're at the mercy of nature, in a wild, archaic landscape. There are many things we can plan in advance: logistics, equipment, partners, etc. But there are always a certain number of unknowns. Nature is ever-changing; no two days are ever the same. You can't reduce nature to a formula. And because it is creative and changeable, I always have to take those changes into account as I go. Usually, they are natural phenomena, such as a sudden drop in temperature or a storm or an insurmountable obstacle – things I couldn't have planned for beforehand. Or we suddenly find we're missing a piece of equipment, or the hazards prove so formidable that we have to run for our lives. Or rather, in our case, abseil down calmly. If you run for it, you won't last long.

Here, then, is an example of the art of stopping as a specific cultural tool. Whereas fear usually triggers a spontaneous flight response, that would be fatal on a mountainside. Therefore the retreat has to be just as careful and considered as the ascent; he who flees, dies. In my view, this adds a new dimension to the concept of stopping: it is not an instantaneous act, as when the office worker drops his pen at 5 pm and clocks off for the day, but a highly complex process that calls for learned skills. This is something we need to take into account in our reflections on stopping. Stopping needs a reason, but the ability to stop takes skill. Messner has translated the principle of stopping into a practical life skill: 'I can talk about stopping on a number of fronts. Six times in my life I have given up something I loved doing in order to start something new. I have gone from rock climber to mountaineer, to extreme mountaineer, to researcher, to museum founder, to filmmaker. And soon I will stop making films and start something else.'

And why? 'Everything you can do to the maximum of your own abilities eventually becomes routine and boring. And life is much more exciting when you have the curiosity to seek new adventures.'

Although my own activities are much closer to ground level than Reinhold Messner's, I could identify with this. Research has only ever interested me to the extent that it helps me answer a particular question – such as how 'perfectly normal' people decide to participate in massacres and mass murder. Or how our autobiographical memory works. I would never have dreamed of devoting my life to researching a particular topic, even though that is the standard model of successful scholarship. I have been a video artist, journalist, gallerist, social scientist, author and exhibition organizer, and it goes without saying that you have to stop doing one thing if you want to start another. In this case, our behaviour is not driven by the fear of doing something – unless you happen to be stuck on the south face of the Dhaulagiri (which, incidentally, has yet to be fully conquered) – but on the contrary, by the fear of not doing it: it's not easy to give up something you've been successful at thus far. After all, you would know what to expect if you kept going, and that you would get by perfectly well. Psychologically speaking, success is the surest way to stagnation, while stopping and starting anew is associated with uncertainty and anxiety. Aversion to change is normal, and therefore we must develop the technique of stopping and starting anew.

One of the most shocking things I have seen in recent years was a queue of over three hundred mountaineers waiting for hours for the chance to stand on the summit of Mount Everest. At several points along the way lay the dead bodies of those who didn't quite make it, and who hadn't yet been removed for logistical reasons. They weren't going to decay in a hurry in those freezing temperatures, after all. It was the ultimate symbol of the empty, cynical process of 'carrying on'. Each of these schizoid self-conquerors had paid a five-figure sum for this adventure of a lifetime; who in such circumstances would stop short of the summit just because they had to queue for a few hours in the presence of their dead colleagues? A macabre metaphor indeed for a cultural credo based on ploughing ahead at any cost.

Aside from his mountaineering feats, Reinhold Messner prides himself on something quite different. He styles himself as a 'minimalist adventurer', explaining:

I haven't given up adventuring, just the use of more and more equipment. My achievement doesn't lie in inventing new technical appliances or developing new technologies. It lies in practising the art of reduction. I was the first to climb Mount Everest without a mask, so I didn't have to have those heavy oxygen cylinders carried up. I was the first to single-handedly conquer an eight thousander with sixty kilos of equipment. Ten years before, I had been on an expedition that took eight tons of gear – that time just as a participant, not the organizer. Reducing the amount of equipment allowed me to shed ballast and become much quicker and more creative, and hence more successful. That's a style of mountaineering that had already been tried by a few climbers before the First World War, but was never pursued. I describe my Alpine-style mountaineering phase as 'abstinence mountaineering'. The goal is no longer to conquer the highest peaks and the hardest approaches, but to tackle the hardest approaches with as few aids as possible.

Another symbol of progress, but this time of the opposite kind: one that lies not in increasing but reducing resources. One that lies in cultivating the cultural tool of 'less not more', as a counterpoint to the traditional notion of progress promoted by our modern consumerist society. The measure of that progress is not volume, but lightness – the shedding of ballast, expenditure, equipment. We should all become abstinence adventurers.

Another abstinence adventurer from a very different walk of life is one I can't call up on the phone, as he has been dead for a few centuries. I'm talking about the person I consider the best and most important painter in history.

Jan Vermeer van Delft

Vermeer lived, from 1632 to 1675, in the city of Delft. He was a contemporary of Pieter de Hooch and Jan Steen, both of whom also lived in Delft and were members of the local Guild of St Luke, of which Vermeer was twice dean. He was (probably) a friend of Anton van Leeuwenhoek, a scientist, microscopist and surveyor already famous at that time, and who is thought to be the subject of Vermeer's painting *The Geographer.* Vermeer was, therefore – by seventeenth-century standards – a well-known artist in his own lifetime whose works sold for significant sums (his paintings fetched up to 200 guilders at auction in 1696, while a Rembrandt went for seven guilders at the same auction), although his private life, which has been variously immortalized on page and screen (*The Girl with the Pearl Earring*), seems to have been plagued by marital and financial troubles.

Much more interesting, however, is the fact that – despite Vermeer's importance in Delft during his lifetime, not just as an artist, but as an art dealer, citizen and dean of the guild – so little is known of his back story. Equally puzzling are two characteristics of his phenomenal *oeuvre*: first, that it comprises a total of just thirty-seven paintings (two of which are of disputed authorship), and second, that he left no drawings, sketches, drafts or overpainted canvases, which is extremely rare. As for the incredible painterly quality of Vermeer's pictures and their radicalism (take the simple fact that the *Girl with the Pearl Earring* is painted – highly unusually for the time – against a monochrome background, for example, or that the (supposed) *Girl Reading a Letter* holds a blank piece of paper in her hands), all we know is that he probably used a camera obscura for some of them; otherwise, it remains a complete mystery how all this could be created without sketches, preliminary drawings or drafts. And why he painted no more than three dozen pictures.

My own theory, which is by no means supported by art scholarship, is that the artist's aim – as always in the case of great art – was to paint the perfect picture: one that was visibly of this world, while at the same time penetrating and transcending it, hinting at a world behind the existing, familiar one. Do go if you can to one of the few museums with a Vermeer and have a look for yourself: you may experience that unique feeling of being unable to tear yourself away. Or, after moving on, of feeling compelled to go back and look at it again – and again. Not, of course, because of the picture's photographic realism. It doesn't show what we know, but what we *don't* know – something whose existence we can only guess at. The picture behind the picture. I think that's what Vermeer was aiming at, and that is something one may be able to achieve in a few works, but not in 150 or 200. And certainly not in sketches and drawings. Hence the fact that the artist, having accomplished a masterpiece that met or went some way towards meeting his own aspirations, ceased painting altogether. Moreover, he will have destroyed any preliminary versions of his work, along with, presumably, all traces and documents of his life – or how else can we explain the fact that we know virtually nothing about a man of such importance in his own lifetime? Perhaps he was motivated by a belief that the vagaries and circumstances of the painter's life are irrelevant to, and a distraction from, the picture itself. As such, Vermeer gives us the picture behind the picture, but no picture in front of the picture.

Interestingly, one of his last works (the pictures are for the most part undated and their titles assigned retrospectively) was first understood as an 'allegory of painting', then later as an allegory of history, with the woman pictured sitting for the portrait being interpreted as Clio, the muse of history. In terms of content, therefore, the picture is about the poetry of history. But more interesting to me is the fact that the painter has painted himself painting. In other words, he produces a (perfect) final reflection of his own craft, full of interpretive

Fig. 2.1: Vermeer, *The Art of Painting*. The last picture?

possibilities and hence unresolved questions – and then he stops. This is, admittedly, a rather free interpretation, as the dating is not certain, but research shows that it was created in the last years of Vermeer's life, so there's a good likelihood that it was the last picture.

And isn't it a great project to paint a last picture, compose a last piece of music or write a last book entirely in the spirit of Reinhold Messner's above-quoted remark: 'Everything you can do to the maximum of your own abilities eventually becomes routine and boring'? Stopping cements your achievement. Continuing banalizes it.

The Art of Painting, as Vermeer's picture is alternatively titled, hangs in Vienna's Kunsthistorisches Museum: do go and see it if you can. The reason why it is housed there, incidentally, is because Adolf Hitler bought it in 1940 for 1,650,000 Reichsmarks in order to secure it for the planned art museum in Linz. Members of the US army later found it in the huge art collection stashed away by the Nazis in the salt mines of Altausee, and handed it over to the Kunsthistorisches Museum. Another story about stopping, but a very different one.

Here's yet another story, and from another time: I am at Berlin's Haus der Festspiele in June 2015 for the theatre and performance festival 'Foreign Affairs'. I have booked for

Tino Sehgal's

This Progress, and I am waiting in the foyer at an appointed time. Suddenly, a very young woman, of seventeen or eighteen perhaps, comes up to me, invites me to walk a little way with her and then asks me how I would define progress. We walk and talk. After a few hundred yards, on a street corner, the woman disappears and the thread is taken up by a man in his late twenties, also very open and friendly. After walking and talking for a few minutes, we reach a crossroads, and a middle-aged woman takes over. And so it goes on until, some twenty or thirty minutes later, I find myself back at the theatre, this time in conversation with an elderly lady. The lady disappears with a friendly farewell, and I am left alone. I am simultaneously confused and moved. Though I must say these are my two most common emotions in any artistic encounter. For me, it's often a physical thing: goosebumps are the surest sign that I am in the presence of great art.

Art is not something we respond to on a cognitive or intellectual level alone, which is why most academic texts on art theory are so mind-numbingly dull. Art is that transcendent phenomenon that resists all cognitive analysis – something that gives you goosebumps, an experience and, later, a memory. The 1976-born artist Tino Sehgal achieves this by creating strange situations like the one I have just described. Strange because we're not generally in the habit of talking to people we don't know – especially about serious issues and while going for a stroll. Strange because we don't normally switch interlocutors without warning, as if cutting to the next scene in a film. And strange because they are ephemeral, leaving no trace but your own memory. The artist expressly refuses to have his works filmed or otherwise documented. They exist only for the duration of the encounter, and they all involve some kind of interaction between the performers and the exhibition-goers, who thus become part of the art project.

And now to Dresden, 2012: around three dozen people are posted around the atrium of the Albertinum art museum. They stand together or alone, talking or singing. Perfectly normal people of different ages and backgrounds. They too speak to the visitors directly, so that the categories are suddenly blurred: what is a visitor, what is an actor in the context of this art project, entitled *These Associations*? Indeed, is there any difference between the two? Won't they all, by the end, have memories of their encounters and a repertoire of stories to tell about them? All Sehgal's works have this same unusual quality, for which he is highly acclaimed in the international art world.

For environmental reasons, Sehgal never flies to his exhibitions, which are staged at the world's top art museums. He prefers to take a cabin on a cargo ship, for example, on the basis that it would be sailing anyway and having an artist on board makes no difference. For Sehgal, this is entirely in keeping with the intangibility of his work as a whole, which can best be described as social choreography. An instance of human interaction that creates its own peculiar beauty and needs no equipment, no budget, and no hard disk or cloud to preserve it for posterity. What's gone is gone. In an interview with German radio, Sehgal explained:

> The issue of transience is of course a key theme. If you asked Plato, he would probably say that ideas are what endures, whereas matter is transient. Or the soul is the thing that remains, whereas the body is ephemeral. Our culture has rather turned this around. I mean, we assume material to be the most substantial thing. The thing that endures. In many cultures, that's not the case. And I can't say I'm really persuaded by the way our culture sees it.[1]

I would agree: I am similarly unpersuaded by the tendency of our culture to prize material things so highly that intangible – and especially transitory – things automatically appear less important than something that is literally tangible, in the form of a product. Yet the artist insists categorically that his works are museum pieces. They can even be purchased as chore-ographies and, in consultation with Sehgal, performed, or rather brought to life. In an interview with a reporter from the German daily *taz*, Sehgal reflects on our concept of progress:

> It is generally the case that our society still defines itself in terms of technological progress: development means the transforma-tion of natural resources into ever more ingenious products thanks to continual technical advances. But we already have far more than we need; besides, this system of production is unsustainable, and also a bit boring. So for me the question was how to oppose this without lapsing into asceticism.[2]

The artist demonstrates a very different kind of progress – one that, without equipment, without the conversion of materials, without an end product, allows a new and uplifting experience of reality. There's nothing ascetic or self-denying about it: quite the contrary. Indeed, the curious pleasure of an unexpected and fleeting encounter is perhaps the defining characteristic of this kind of progress. This art isn't *meant* to endure and, as such, maybe it offers another training exercise in the art of stopping: let us all collect moments and experiences that were beautiful, or overwhelmingly so, for the moment or duration of their existence or occurrence, and examine our memory to see if a trace of that beauty still remains. And then let us see how this compares with the value of, say, an Audi Q8.

Realities:united

Have we discussed the business of leave taking yet? An important and much-underestimated phenomenon. We are generally reluctant to part with things – a hometown, a person, a beloved object. And particularly something we have done for a long time. But sometimes we have no choice, and then there are the usual rituals – hugs, shared tears, a farewell dinner, a leaving party or ceremony. But the restless modern age has no ritual for parting from things that have been important to it, and it may be that we cling all the more tightly to objects for which there is no valedictory protocol. When a factory is demolished, it is done without ceremony. When coal-fired power stations are shut down, there is no fanfare. But might the transition to a new phase, the switch to a new strategy, prove much easier if there were a ritual to accompany the act of stopping? After all, there are rites of passage in other cultural contexts: confirmations, proms, weddings, baptisms, burials. But when it comes to changing to a new energy regime, for example, there is just a decision – and that's it. Before the event, there are protracted negotiations over exit strategies, severance schemes and so on, but there is no 'after the event'. Nothing.

Power stations are emblems of the industrial age.[3] For a long time, smokestacks and cooling towers were positive symbols of progress and growing prosperity. Not even smoke – despite its extremely harmful effects on health, particularly in the early days of industrialization – was considered a bad thing: on the contrary, the smoking chimney stood for labour, growth and national superiority. And the miners who supplied the fuel, and later the engineers who developed the fuel rods for nuclear power plants, were hailed as the energy source of an upwardly mobile society. They were celebrated, not demonized.

As already noted, improved living standards for people in emerging economies, the rapid growth of the middle classes, the rise of consumer cultures, increased wealth, higher mobility and better health and education are prime examples of the double-edged nature of the growth-based economy. Because the two trends go hand in hand: as average living standards rise, so does the rate of destruction of our natural resources.

This duality of progress and destruction is not something we like to talk about. We prefer to emphasize the progress side of things, from the replacement of old technologies with new ones through the aspiration to 'decarbonize' the entire economy to the declaration of 'energy revolutions' and the 'greening' of everything from our food supply to the financial industry. That said, the controversies over wind farms and power lines are a clear sign that there is far less identification with the new technologies than with the old. In Germany, this has set politicians panicking over the voting behaviour of disgruntled miners in the coal-producing heartland of Lusatia, and offering billions in subsidies in an attempt to pacify them. That attempt is hardly likely to succeed, however, as no amount of money can compensate for the symbolic devaluation and nullification of labour, expertise and identity.

This is yet another instance of the failure of modernity, with its unconditional belief in progress, to recognize the category of finitude. Its concept of progress is a continuous expansion of world share and world domination; contraction and retreat have no place in this vision, nor does the cessation of a trend that has had its day. This can render technological progress so blind that no one stops to reflect that energy regimes are also energy cultures – in other words, that our fossil-fuelled culture has also spawned its very own cultural identity that cannot give up its fossil heritage without pain.

The fact is that a deep connection and mutual relationship have evolved here. Energy production, like other basic infra-structures, is no longer simply an essential service but has long become bound up in all sorts of ways with the existence and identity of society in general and specific groups in particular. One recent CDU party chairman built his campaign speech around his father's mining background, and it would be hard to find a clearer example of the persistence of a bygone industrial culture. Energy, it seems, is much more than just a corollary of labour and prosperity: it is integral to our very being and existence and, moreover, an outward symbol of a vision of individual and social development.

There are multiple interconnected levels of impact here, and it makes sense to reflect and organize the infrastructure of energy generation on each of those levels. Just as the physical processes themselves require an engineered control system and a management system for the organizational and commercial aspects, so the parallel production of meaning and significance and the symbols associated with it should be taken seriously as an area in its own right and managed accordingly. Aesthetics matter here, as the perception of importance often coincides with the perception of creative beauty, power or elegance.

The conflicts around the new wind farms are a case in point. Although the structures are elegant and quite remarkable in themselves, they often find little favour with the public. This is probably partly because – unlike in mining – there is no large-scale industrial culture attached to wind generation, and hence little scope for identity building in the places where the turbines are installed and operated. There are no local work-forces to assign meaning and value to them, if only for the sake of their own livelihood. Yet the factual arguments in favour of this technology are strong, and its actual negative impacts and risks are low by comparison with other infrastructures, industries or agriculture.

What is most striking about the opposition to wind power, however, is that it is not based on risks or economic argu-ments, but on perceived visual impact and noise pollution – on sensory factors, in other words. This shows how important it is for a technology to be seen as coherent on every level, from the technical through the economic to the overarching level of symbolic significance and the specific aesthetic associated with it.

The same is true in the opposite case: that is, when a tech-nology is to be phased out. The success of such a venture depends on how well the associative context can be dismantled and reinterpreted – in other words, whether it is possible to destroy the physical structure of an old power station without it being automatically perceived as the destruction of a set of values and way of life.

In such situations, rituals can help to shape the decline or destruction of the material legacy in such a way that the identity-building, ideational legacy is hived off and preserved, and its value perhaps even enhanced, as in the ceremonial and 'dignified' setting of a funeral or burial. Here the deceased can be honoured as a *person*, while their body is cremated or buried. The same goes for sacred buildings slated for demoli-tion. In this case, the ritualized process of profanation serves to separate the ideational aspect of religion from the building itself, so as to avoid the impression that the associated beliefs are being similarly bulldozed.

What we need, therefore, is a formalized valedictory process to accompany the phasing out of major technologies on which many decades of industrial culture and many generations of individual lives have depended. Yet no such thing exists, and this is where the project Fazit comes in – a kind of farewell gesture to an energy culture that has imprinted itself not just on the landscape, in the form of chimneys and cooling towers, but also on people's everyday lives. Fazit is a project of realities:united, a group of artists and architects founded by the brothers

Jan and Tim Edler

The idea of thematizing smoke as a side effect of energy production came about in connection with a competition won by realities:united in 2011. Proposals had been invited for the new waste-to-energy plant Amagerforbrænding in Copenhagen, and the architecture firm BIG had entered a design incorporating the plant into an artificial mountain and using the roof as a 31,000-square-metre ski park with runs for all levels of ability. The idea was to turn a building with generally unpleasant associations – a waste incinerator – into something positive – a recreation area. Realities:united proposed that the emissions from the incineration process be modulated by a special device

Fig. 2.2:   The poetry of waste incineration

in the smokestack so that they would be blown into the sky as single smoke rings.

Besides creating a poetic visual effect, this would provide a kind of index via which Copenhageners could measure their waste and hence their CO_2 production: the more waste they generated and fed into the incineration plant, the more smoke rings would be emitted, each containing and representing half a ton of CO_2.

In the event, the Copenhagen project didn't come to fruition, but the same approach was transferred to a new object: the addition of an artistic dimension to the regular output of a power plant. The implicit cultural message that power plants already send out by their very nature would be made an explicit part of the installation. The scene of the action would be the large collection of power plants in Germany that have either been decommissioned or earmarked for decommissioning: their cooling tower function would be adapted so as to produce large smoke rings as a visible symbol of a farewell ritual lasting for years. By harnessing the Bernoulli effect, the smoke ring-emitting cooling towers would be turned into symbols of farewell to our fossil-fuelled energy culture.

The Bernoulli effect, named after its discoverer Daniel Bernoulli (1700-1782), is another term for the so-called hydrodynamic paradox, whereby a low-pressure zone is generated around a fast-flowing (gas) stream. When a gas such as steam emerges from a pipe into the air, a ring of low pressure is formed around the outlet. The escaping steam is pulled towards this low-pressure zone and hence deflected outwards. Under certain conditions, the steam is sucked right into the vortex ring, which is eventually released from the outlet. This produces an isolated ring of steam that moves through the air. Once generated, such free-floating vortex rings are remarkably stable and durable. This phenomenon is also found in nature: on Mount Etna in Sicily, smoke rings have been observed with a diameter of up to 200 metres and a visibility of up to ten minutes.

Fig. 2.3:   Retired power plant, gently smoking

Such a gesture would be both aesthetically impactful and historically appropriate, honouring both the subjective energy of the workforce and the progress achieved in the past. What's more, the project takes an existing landmark and gives it a resonance evocative not only of the everyday problem of emissions but also of the wider theme of transience: a historical epoch dissolving into a cloud of vapour.

At each location, the series of smoke signals rising into the sky will create a concrete and worthy signal of impending shutdown. As we transition to clean energy, the 'concert' of all the plants, extending across the entire country over a period of 20 years, will serve as a symbol and visualization of the entire shutdown or switchover process and the radical transformation of the technical infrastructure, values and attitudes behind it.

The purpose of Fazit, therefore, is to enable Germany's major nuclear or fossil-fuelled power plants to stage a coordinated farewell performance in the final years leading up to their demise: the choreographed end of a long and great era of the industrial age. In addition to energy production, the slightly modified plants will now take on another function: making beautiful, high-flying clouds. In synchrony throughout the land. Visible from afar, from Lusatia in the east to the Lower Rhine in the west. Locations and regions that have been shaped by their role as energy producers on the outskirts of the country's urban centres will be visibly connected. Because an opportunity like this will never come again.

With this project, Jan and Tim Edler have managed to integrate the concept of stopping into the cultural landscape, which is why its implementation is so urgently necessary. The Edlers are experts in coming up with amazing ideas which appear unrealistic when first mooted. Another striking example is the Flussbad Berlin, which aims to transform the Spree Canal into a 700-metre-long swimming pool in the centre of Berlin, between the Pergamon Museum and the reconstructed Stadtschloss – right on the axis of Prussian global influence. Needless to say, the idea of people in swimming trunks and bikinis swimming around in a place where (simulated) history and (perceived) historic grandeur are presented for the edification of international tourists is a nightmare for traditionalists and fans of high culture.

Despite this, after much wrangling and public debate, the Flussbad is now in a concrete planning and execution phase – something no one would have initially believed possible. (I should add that I am an enthusiastic member of the advisory board of the Flussbad Berlin Association, hence the plug.)

And now for something completely different. Someone who springs to mind as a person who has done a great many – and at first sight strange – things in their life, is

Johannes Heimrath

Musician, instrument maker, founder and publisher of several magazines, rediscoverer of early music, co-founder of living and working communities, experimenter in alternative life-styles, book author, local politician and probably much else besides. Central to Heimrath's thinking today is the connectedness of all life, and it is most instructive to listen to and discuss with him his reflections on the affinity between human life and all forms of what he calls 'parahuman life'.

I remember one occasion at a conference organized by my foundation FUTURZWEI ('Future Perfect') when he suddenly placed a rather sickly-looking house plant in the middle of the room and asked the participants to incorporate it into their contributions to the debate; it was interesting how the atmosphere changed after that. Someone who co-founded an eco-village that has existed for more than a quarter of a century and who lives apart from the mainstream is bound to be an interesting person to talk to on the subject of stopping, I thought, and indeed, it was almost like a rerun of my conversation with Reinhold Messner. Like Messner, Johannes talked of all the occupations and activities he had begun and given up during his life, and for the same reason as Messner:

> I have always stopped doing a particular thing at the point when I thought: I can't improve on this. As a musician, I thought: 'If I carry on making music, it won't get any better than this.' There's a certain moment after which it just becomes routine. And what's the point of carrying on after that? All you're doing is exploiting that skill. You could become a cash cow and live

off your success for ever after. But I'm not made for that, it's just not me.

Instead, Heimrath is a serial starter and stopper.

Part of his motivation, if I understand him rightly, is to find answers to specific questions via experimentation: questions such as whether the eco-lobby is right that we could reduce our 'ecological footprint' to a sustainable, globally manageable and equitable level. For Johannes, these are not questions that can be answered with theory. On the land he farms with the village community, they are a concrete reality – when a 50-hp tractor simply isn't up to the job, for instance, and you need a more powerful one. Or when installing a solar farm absorbs so much material and energy that it takes decades for the thing to pay for itself.

Heimrath's (in my eyes) hard-core eco-village Klein Jasedow is, essentially, a great experiment aimed at deconstructing the myths of the sustainability discourse in a practical way. And it's not about being proved right:

> The question we ask ourselves is this: if it doesn't work, how *might* it work? And for that you need a certain amount of courage to get over the ideological obstacles. You have to have machines, tools, machines for making machines. The question is, how do we bring this machinery back within the planetary boundaries? How much of a technosphere do we need? And what kind of lifestyle would that require?

For Heimrath, it's not about romanticism but about taking our historically evolved fractality seriously and finding ways to break out of our apparent path dependency and obsession with consistency – quite literally, to cut a swathe through it.

> On a piece of land you can clear a space to do your own thing. We are becoming a model workshop for subsistence farming, so

we can ask in real terms: what do we need to stop doing? What steps are essential before we can even think about stopping? When we talk about scaling down technology, we're talking 50 hp for the smallest tractor. But I need more than 50 hp to prepare this ground and reverse the sins of industrial farming. I can't escape the trap of fractality. And the next challenge is: do I have to be so ascetic about these things? Or is there a fuzzy area? Can I commit a sin in one place if I compensate for it in another? Dogma won't get you anywhere.

Klein Jasedow is one big learning curve which has nothing to do with orthodoxy. The musical instrument workshop, which specializes in gongs, is a conventional business, as is the sustainable agriculture project. As such, the eco-village is inexorably bound up with capitalism and that makes it realistic: an experiment working within the familiar status quo. But it is one in which alternative spaces, new realms of possibility, can be explored. For Johannes Heimrath, the categories of uniqueness, unrepeatability, sufficiency, are hugely important in this context. He talks about the 'exemplary day' – one in which something perfect happens: a conversation, a piece of music, a fleeting instant of wholeness:

> Once you have experienced something like that, you don't need to look any further. You don't need to relive it. The metaphor is real: it opens up a new quality of life. If you are willing to let it stand as a one-off event. The intensity of sensation, the power of the unique. After that, you can die happy. Irretrievability: that's an indispensable ingredient when it comes to quality of experience.

What matters, then, is not the attempt to recapture the moment but the appreciation of the moment itself. So it's no surprise that Heimrath has something to say about death. Within the village community, end-of-life support is something perfectly normal, and the last breath of the dying a familiar experience.

> With all those we have supported over the past few years, you could always recognize the moment of their last breath. You think the one before is the last, but when the final one comes, you know it. Even then, you're still not dead. It's only after that last outbreath that the dying processes begin to kick in. So there is still a degree of consciousness – in fact there are traditions associated with this whole phenomenon. In my mother's case, it struck me that this is the deepest connection we have as human beings. One day it will be my last breath too. That's something we all share. That seemed much more significant to me than the other thing we all share: the experience of birth, or rather being born. The act of departing this world, the going away – perhaps it has to do with the fact that birth brings us into a world already familiar to the living, whereas death takes us into the unknown. And in that moment of my mother's last breath, that deep commonality seemed particularly meaningful to me.

Heimrath has an alternative view of death: not as the end of everything, but merely the dissolution of that specific combination of substances and materials that we call human life. Since carbon atoms for example – like all other atoms – don't die but are re-embodied elsewhere, the decay of the human body is not the end of its constituent substances. This thought leads Heimrath to reflect that, as living beings, our bodies are already recycling systems, since each of our atoms existed before us, only in other forms. What he finds astonishing is that, 'If I am one big recycling system, then surely it's time I started addressing that materiality. It's not just death that I will undergo – it's a whole process of degradation that is never really over. It's just borrowed substance that goes on to make up other entities.'

In this way, Heimrath links birth and death together as two different forms of the same process:

> There is a last moment after which the growth vector is reversed. The biological units break down. Growth begins with fertilization. There ought to be a bridge from one to the other. From the moment of conception, an autopoietic process begins in which you can't say: job done. And in that sense, that last breath ... there was something similar about it, there's a moment when ... how can I put it? Language isn't enough, it would be easier to express it in music. It's not just the deep commonality. It's almost as if life has taken a risk by bringing this person into being. You've gone through your whole life facing all kinds of risks, but that pales into insignificance beside the question: why did life hazard this being?

Looked at this way, the interval between birth and death is actually irrelevant. It doesn't matter *how long* a person's life lasts: the important thing for Heimrath seems to be the role of that person's 'hazarded' life within the web of relationships with all other life forms.

> When I talk about commonality, I don't just mean the life we human beings enjoy. We share it with all other living beings too, of course – that's the point at which all life converges. And then there is this bridge whereby your life can only function if you take other lives. I mean eating, breathing, walking – all of this is fatal to other lives. Only they are so damn tiny you're not aware of them. The tree is part of me, and I am part of it. There's nothing esoteric about that, just the plain fact that all living processes are interconnected. There is no such thing as independent life. All living entities are dependent on one another. That's a physical and biological reality, pure and simple.

You could describe Johannes Heimrath's project as an attempt to abolish the divisions that define our modern world view. To me, there is something disconcerting about this, but that's precisely what I find interesting. The idea that a life is not simply something given, but something hazarded, has two implications. First, the sheer improbability of being born as the person you are – a notion akin to Hannah Arendt's concept of natality. And, second, the ability of that hazarded – in the sense of open-ended, unfinished, incomplete – entity to become a self that does or doesn't do something, or allows or causes something to be done. This indeterminacy of life is independent of the measurable phenomenon of lifespan; it has meaning in and of itself. Therein lies, in my view, what Arendt calls the 'responsibility for the world' that shows that 'men, though they must die, are not born in order to die'.[4] This (if you'll pardon the neologism) dequantifies the time between birth and death, removing it from the realm of the countable.

Which brings me to one of the most impressive people I have ever met.

Katja Baumgarten

Katja and I go back a long way. We were at school together, and at one stage she went out with my best friend, with whom I shared a flat in my early student days. After leaving school, Katja first trained as a midwife, then went on to study art and subsequently became a filmmaker. In both professions, she has had much to do with the existential themes of this book, making her an obvious person to talk to. Her first film, released in 1992, was entitled *Grandfather – Where Am I From, Where Am I Going?* and showed her interacting with her then 94-year-old grandfather. This early work was already characterized by an unusual mixture of tenderness and acerbity – something that really comes across when you watch it. It made no bones about the restrictions that such a ripe old age imposes, while at the same time showing how the old man insisted on his independence and tried – not without success – to assert himself against his granddaughter. Put it this way: it is a film which, once seen, is not easily forgotten. Not a film about stopping but about a life approaching its end.

The film that brought Katja wider recognition was called *My Little Baby*; after premiering in 2002, it was screened in many cinemas and appeared many times on German television from 2003 onwards, generating a great deal of debate. It is about a pregnant woman who is told after a scan that her baby has a 'complex malformation syndrome', meaning that it would be born severely disabled and with a very short life expectancy. The prognosis, it seems, is 'very poor'. The woman is in the twenty-first week of her pregnancy, and the 'customary procedure' after such a diagnosis is, according to the doctor, 'to terminate the pregnancy'.

The woman in question is the filmmaker herself, and the film shows what happens after this diagnosis. As is also customary, the doctor leaves the decision of whether or not to terminate to the shocked mother: 'It's up to you.' As already pointed out, however, the custom in such cases is to abort, especially given the risks that continuing to term would pose to the mother during both pregnancy and birth. But a premature induced birth in mid-term also brings risks for the mother, as a midwife well knows. Ultimately, the mother decides to defy 'custom' and see the thing through. The film shows the pregnancy, birth and death of the child. It does all this without spectacle or pathos, and with a naturalness not usually associated with such a life and death. The whole thing takes place in an atmosphere of normality that the filmmaker herself creates, having once decided against an abortion and in favour of a home birth (such normality being impossible to achieve in a hospital setting). And the presence of Katja's other three children is very much part of that. As Katja recalls:

That phrase of the doctor's, 'It's up to you' was key to the whole film. And I told the doctor there and then, even though everything was collapsing around my ears, that I would bring my camerawoman with me to the next appointment. It was crazy, I was in shock, and I just felt, I've got to record this. Hearing that I didn't have a healthy baby, and the next minute having to take the decision to end its life! It was such a surreal experience, I thought: I need to document this. I didn't originally plan to make a film of it – I just wanted to have a record of it all. The impulse to make the film – a lot of people said it was a way of working through my grief, but it wasn't that. It was as if I still had a bone to pick with this society. You're still reeling from the shock, and the next thing they tell you is that 'you need to consider whether you'll be able to cope. In most cases, the baby doesn't survive.' I felt I wanted to use the film to pass on my life experience and open up the discussion again. That was what prompted me to persevere with it over the years. It was a real long-term project. Martin was born in 1997, that's when we did the recording, and the film was released in 2002. So I let it marinate for a long time. And I needed breaks in between. Plus I had my children to think about.

To give you a flavour, here is an extract from the film diary published on Katja's home page:

Saturday 28 June
No energy today.
Last night Paula asks me in the hallway, in front of Niki:
    'How are you feeling, mum?'
    'Awful,' I say, 'couldn't be worse.'
I tell them that our little baby is very poorly, that it will
    die when it's born – or at least be very poorly once it's
    out of my tummy.

We stand in the hallway, me hugging them both.

Then on the sofa in the kitchen – Nikolaus on my right, huddled up to me, Paula on my left, Michael playing.

I tell them about the scan.

That the baby's heart hasn't grown properly, and a few other things besides.

I don't tell them yet that it doesn't have fully formed arms.

Instead, I tell them the doctor said it's doing fine in my tummy, that it's not in pain and is cosy in there.

Paula asks whether there's any hope, whether the doctor might be mistaken and things might turn out OK –

I say no.

I say that the ultrasound doctor told me there was a 50 per cent chance of it being born alive – though it will always be seriously ill – and that I don't expect it will have to stay in hospital all the time.

Nikolaus doesn't say much.

'It's not fair that some people get to live a long time and others don't', he says.

They have just been doing the Middle Ages at school.

The cruel punishments in those days have made an impression on him.

He can't believe that killing an unborn, sick baby is allowed in this day and age.

Later, Paula says: 'Mum, if there's any risk to you, you *will* have to have an abortion – the three of us need you too.'

Aborting a baby with 'multiple malformations' is the socially expected thing to do: the choice facing a pregnant woman in this situation is not really a choice at all. The doctor and the society in which he operates make it clear that they expect Katja to opt for a termination. She doesn't see herself as a pregnant woman, however, but as a mother faced with the decision of ending her baby's life.

Despite being in what she describes as a state of utter distress and feeling 'at her wits' end' over the following days, it is important to her to document those emotions. From then on, therefore, she makes continuous recordings, which she later turns into the film *My Little Baby*. It is a film that not only raises the issue of prenatal diagnosis and its consequences from a first-hand perspective, but also opens up a space beyond the social expectations around pregnancy termination. Because Katja decides to give birth to her baby. And she talks to her other children about it:

> A lot of people said, you're treating them like mini adults! Because I told the children very early on what was wrong. I didn't just invent some story but told them the facts. And they reacted in a much more mature, normal way than many adults. They really got it. They had heard the heartbeats and had already . . . their little sibling was already part of our family. Of course, I wasn't sure at first what to do – it wasn't as if I felt: I have endless reserves, I'll get through this. I had no idea what to do in that situation. And then Nikolaus immediately took the baby's part, whereas Paula said, 'We mustn't lose you as well.' She was more worried about me.

Nikolaus is twelve at this stage, Paula ten. And then there is three-year-old Michael. The presence of the children in the film seems so natural that the viewer is initially taken aback – indeed, its very power lies in the fact that it presents an extremely difficult situation as one that can still be managed even if you don't follow the expected norms. It is well worth a watch as it deals with something that is usually not even talked about – not in a confrontational way, but in a manner that is deeply touching, precisely because it is ultimately a film about life. As such, the children are part of everything else that happens, right up to the birth and death of baby Martin:

They were there during and after the birth and said goodbye to him, and there was a kind of normality about it all. It sounds silly, but that's how it was. And afterwards there was a sort of calm that became part of our life. It was a sad time too, of course, but that really acute grief was at the beginning, in that traumatic time when I thought, I'm in a trap and don't know where to turn. Later, we were all more relieved than anything to have got through it. And I felt the children had dealt with it well. We even celebrated Martin's birthday for a few years afterwards. When my grandparents died, the children were involved again, helping to decorate the coffin and so on. Life goes on; everyone has their time. When an arc is completed and something is accomplished, that's not stopping. It's completion. There's a difference.

Katja doesn't see death in terms of stopping, but as the end of a linear progression that begins with birth. The stream of life only flows in one direction, she says, and when it's over, 'it's no longer linear, but rounded off.' Not like a circle, she adds, but three-dimensional, like a ball. Language can't do justice to feelings like this; her meaning, she says, is better expressed 'non-linguistically'. But I understand nevertheless. And, above all, I understand that this quality of completion has nothing to do with how long a life lasts. This is the central message of *My Little Baby*: life is not something that can be measured or rated in terms of duration. That's hard to accept when our death notices are full of phrases such as 'all too soon' and 'snatched from this life'. Is it right that a long life should automatically be considered more fulfilling than a short one?

That was the lesson baby Martin taught me. My grandfather lived to ninety-seven; what is such a 'short' life in comparison? As if it wasn't worth living. But my feeling at the time was: OK, he's only with us for a short while, so we'll make it as good as we can. I want him to have the best time, and us to have the best time with him. And when I look back and see what that ostensibly short life inspired – the inspiration for me to make the film, and the number of people who have responded to it, it's had a real ripple effect. And I still meet people today who saw the film back then. Perhaps you don't need a long life to start a ball rolling: perhaps he only needed a short lifespan for his form of inspiration, for what he brought to the world as an inspiration to others. Even then, the idea of 'the longer, the better' seemed misguided to me. After all, I saw from my grandfather how hard a long life can be.

Accordingly, Katja doesn't regard her midwifery as a service, but as a supporting and protecting role that helps make life possible. 'The journey from birth onwards only goes in one direction, and I see it as my job to safeguard these special moments. I am there to offer support and protection along the way.' Nearly three decades ago now, Katja helped bring our own son into the world, so I know exactly what she means, despite her repeated insistence that it can't be expressed in words. We had a good laugh when I reminded her of a ticking off she gave me back then over some careless action of mine. Neither of us could remember what it was.

In the end, what we're talking about is life – no more, no less. That needs no explanation, nor does it need categories such as spirituality, faith or piety. 'It doesn't matter to me what you call it. I have no religious beliefs to fall back on, so I have to find my own way.' And that she has done in both her professions, as filmmaker and midwife.

Shortly before my conversation with Katja, I met up with another friend, the composer

Thomas Kessler

one of the foremost avant-garde composers, famous for his role in the development of electronic music. A musician ought to have something to say about stopping, I thought, and I was right:

> Stopping is something we constantly have to do. My teacher, Boris Blacher, used to tell me: 'Remember, you must have a good beginning and a good ending. What happens in between is not so important.' I took that advice very seriously – also in relation to the audience. The beginning serves to make them sit up and take notice, and the ending to show them what they were waiting for. Listening to other colleagues' work, I've often thought, hmm, this bit isn't so good, but then it finished on a high. The composer has to work at the ending. I don't know any pieces that just stop randomly. I've never seen a score with an instruction to do that. No, all composers give some thought to the ending. How shall I finish it, how do I make it special? And it's often the case that I think of an ending for a piece while I'm still composing it, and I think: yes, better save that till last. Keep my powder dry for the grand finale.

As with many aesthetic processes, the author has to think of the ending before they get there, be it a play, novel or film. And it's the ending that resonates afterwards, making you think or go back and listen again.

'What are the ingredients of a good ending?' I ask. 'That's a great mystery', he replies.

> If I knew, I'd be very famous. There are fantastic endings that fade down to nothing. That's wonderful. And there are endings that crescendo right up to a fortissimo – a bit crasser, and easier to write. They can be very effective though. As for the ingredients, well, the ending has to confound expectations. The best ending is one you've never heard before. That doesn't mean it necessarily has to be a surprise. It can also be that special moment when you think, yes, that's it!

So there we have it: an ending, a finale, has to be good – the thing towards which all the effort is directed and which has never before been achieved: the conclusion never before heard. This is the reverse of our customary attitude: usually, we *don't* want the end to come, and its associations are accordingly negative. In our cultural model, the end is something to be avoided at all costs, yet in the arts, it plays a key role. And a 'good ending' is not some kind of mechanical template: it has to arise organically from the piece itself, though without – if possible – having been heard before. In this sense, people who work in aesthetic occupations like Thomas Kessler simply have more scope than all those whose job is to deliver predefined products and outcomes.

The ending can come as a surprise, partly of course because a concert, as a collectively realized product, can't be predetermined to the letter anyway.

> Why do I compose? It's friendships that have enriched my life as a composer. I don't think there is any other profession where you have such special relationships with people as in music. It's that shared hope that your concert will go well. The attempt, despite a variety of viewpoints, to understand each other. To put all your energies into producing something good, and bringing it to a successful conclusion.

Sound advice, and a much-needed adjustment of perspective. As we saw, our cultural model naturally encourages a view of the world – and particularly of ourselves – in which we are all separate individuals and, as such, have sole causal agency. But concerts – just like football matches or conversations – are proof that everything we make or do is, on closer examination, the product of collective action based on mutual dependency. And when people act collectively, the outcome is not fixed. In a sense, it will be new and unexpected for everyone. Thus death, too, could be regarded as a collectively rehearsed ending and, as such, would lose much of its wildness.

For Thomas, however, death already holds no fear. He is eighty-three and has lived for two years with the knowledge that he has cancer. His prognosis was three months, but luckily for him a drug has slowed the progress of the disease.

> I don't really want to talk about my wretched illness. Two years ago I was told, you've got three months left. And a doctor on the ward, who also had a penchant for music and knew I was a composer, said don't put yourself through any more, no scans, no check-ups, no biopsies, just make the most of these three months. To him, quitting wasn't an option: when you're given a chance, you shouldn't just drop everything.
>
> That was one of those stopping situations. I lost all interest in death long ago. I have come to think of it like a piece of music – it will just stop. It may stop gradually or all of a sudden. That said, I'm very religious at heart. I am capable of believing. But as for what comes after – I think it's simply the end. And that's wonderful. I won't have to face the ordeal of living in a paradise with bits missing. Or mourning the people I have lost. No, it will all just stop, and therefore there has to be a meaning to the time before. And once it has stopped, none of that will matter any more. That's my very simple philosophy. But it works even in a situation as serious as mine. I didn't think about death. Only about stopping. I thought, I must put the three months left to me to very good use.

With anything that has to stop, it's what happens before that matters: that's a rule of life. The culturally instilled and learned focus on a goal that lies forever out of reach, the continually renewed yet never realized promise of infinity is, it seems, a red herring. The very fact that something has to stop means that the 'Before' is the space we really need to utilize and fill, not the fictional 'Away-from-here'. At last, there is a clear and valid answer to the question of whether there is life after death: there is life *before* death. And *only* before.

I thought about the whole business of stopping. If it's really going to stop now, this little life, then what matters most from a human point of view, which people are dear to me? But it was hard to decide what mattered most. I didn't know, so I just carried on living from day to day. But less superficially than before. When I could tell it wasn't going to be over in three months, and that the drug really was working, I told myself: there are a few things you have to change. Perhaps everyone has a preordained moment, a time when they are ready. Perhaps fate is giving me the strength or the opportunity to carry on a bit longer. But I must use that time very wisely. And that's good. Of course there are things you don't want to stop. A good relationship, for example, where we can't determine and arrange the ending in advance, as in a symphony. Here, too, the time before the end is more important than the end itself.

Sitting opposite Thomas and talking to him like this, you would never dream you were dealing with an old, sick man. The impression of vitality and wisdom he exudes makes questions of age and death seem irrelevant, and this fits with what he calls his strategy of self-deception – his new way of calculating time:

De facto, I will be eighty-four this year. But according to my calculations I will be eighty-eight. That's a good age. How do I do it? By counting each year threefold. It's a con, but a nice con. If you decide at eighty-two that you're going to make each year worth three, then the next year you will be eighty-five and the next eighty-eight. That's a decent age. What's old Kessler got to complain about? Nothing.

Thomas has a few other tricks besides that he uses to stretch time, but I have promised him not to reveal them. Not that he is really deceiving anyone – either himself or others: he merely has a different definition of time. And, miraculously, his ruse really does change the nature of time and its availability. Instead of running away with us, it expands, makes space. There is poetry in this, and a new freedom. The limit we are wont to shrink from – to the point of denial – loses all its terror. Time is on our side.

Time also plays an important part in the life of

Christiane zu Salm

who has a remarkable story to tell. By her early thirties, she was one of Germany's leading female media entrepreneurs and already a public figure, appearing in the colour supplements of newspapers and magazines. She was also an art collector, sat on the advisory and management boards of multiple companies and taught university courses on media management: in a word, she was one of those high-flyers who make you wonder how on earth they manage to do it all on top of having children and probably maintaining an ordinary domestic life as well. In 2016, she bought Nicolai Verlag, a company with a long tradition of publishing political books.

We first met at an election party. At the time, I didn't know much about her history as a successful media entrepreneur – and nothing at all about her other, much more recent career. As I had read in an interview aptly entitled 'You Don't Cry in a Porsche',[5] she is now, following a personal crisis and a long struggle with her own life story, a carer for the terminally ill. In this context, she has also conducted interviews with people who know they are going to die and published them in a book.[6] She has a podcast entitled *Before It's Too Late*. I decide to talk to her, and she tells me about her training as a hospice care assistant:

The training prepares you for interacting with people who know that they haven't got long to live. And the literally wonderful thing about this job is the almost childlike pleasure it gives the dying to know that someone is interested in them and willing to spend time with them – the most precious gift we have! Especially at a time when they appear to have no further role to play, when they no longer wear a social mask – in other words, when it no longer matters what they do or say because it has no impact on their social environment. Yet there is so much beauty in this apparent uselessness. In fact, such an encounter is of course anything but useless, because when an external path is no longer possible, then our task as hospice care assistants is to open up an inner one. An inner path that allows the person to let go of the things, the issues, the thoughts and the pains they carry around with them and make peace with themselves.

Here Christiane zu Salm makes the point that, in normal circumstances, our attitude to and treatment of others is partly instrumental. A person may be important and useful for the future of a friendship, job or network. This is not the only source of our interest in others, but it invariably plays a greater or lesser part in it. When someone no longer has any personal future because their death is certain, they have nothing more to offer from an instrumental perspective – from then on, it is as if their role within their social sphere has been cancelled. Yet Christiane sees this as an exceptional opportunity, as it allows conversations to take place outside the conventional context of instrumentalization and utility. The beauty of these conversations is that they have a value *in themselves* rather than just a pragmatic purpose.

Of course, all conversations of this kind are also about missed opportunities – things that life has denied the dying person, or that they have denied themselves:

All the subjunctives, all the unlived experiences, those typical 'if onlys'. The job of end-of-life caregivers is to open up that space. And it's an extremely valuable space on a human level, because everything that the dying have to say while they are still able to is a great gift to the living – we who are still in a position to change our lives and pursue external paths.

The end of life is a time for reviewing and taking stock, in a way that never happens in our future-oriented lifestyle, with its driven, ceaseless activity. Death is neither present in life, nor is there an art of preparing for it. As we saw earlier, death is not culturally embedded in life: it is the Other – something to be postponed and avoided at all costs. As Christiane zu Salm reflects:

> We live in an age where the culture of death we knew two hundred years ago, with its death knells and rituals, no longer exists because advances in medical technology are all about staying alive, keeping the body going – more tubes, less soul. I have supported coma patients languishing in a hospice for eight years, fed through a drip, because no one wanted to switch off the machines. That's how our society operates – always onwards and upwards, always hanging on doggedly to life. But the art of bowing out . . . that's something we lack.

Many decades ago, two American sociologists, Barney Glaser and Anselm Strauss, produced a famous study entitled *Awareness of Dying*.[7] This was one of my most well-thumbed books in my student days because the authors – after many intensive observations in hospitals and surgeries, as well as interviews with doctors, relatives and care staff – present the surprising conclusion that even the dying are subject to social expectations. They must cooperate with the nurses and refrain from asking the wrong questions, yet at the same time they must refuse to accept their fate and fight their illness and impending death. I found this extremely interesting at the time, as you would have thought that people who are facing their own death already have a hard enough time and therefore ought to be cut some slack. But the opposite is true: even dying has to be regulated and orderly, and patients must conform to a subtly choreographed set of expectations on the part of relatives, hospital management, nursing staff and doctors. To this day, death notices are full of set phrases to this effect ('lost the battle with cancer', and so on), and the idea of departing this life somehow reconciled to death still strikes us as an aberration. We see this attitude reflected in the social condemnation of suicide (on which Thomas Macho has written a very thoughtful book[8]), but also in the public expectation that the dying should not give up but resist death with all their might. Why though, when it is an inevitable fact? Is there any sense in resisting a foregone conclusion? Does it make our exit any easier? For Christiane zu Salm, 'That's where the art of stopping comes in. To become aware and actually register and accept that it's over. That's something we are inherently incapable of doing and find so difficult because death is the last remaining limit in an age when all other limits have been abolished.'

End-of-life care is a craft that has to be learnt.

For example, when someone says: 'I'm scared, I'm really scared of dying', then the worst thing you can say in reply is: 'Don't be!' In fact, that's the worst way to respond to any kind of fear, and particularly existential fear. Why? Because fear is a very basic emotion that we must learn to accept, not suppress. Because all the unresolved issues that occupy us on our deathbed are a result of our fear-driven decisions. Avoiding conflict with someone, failing to have it out with someone and bring about a reconciliation – all these things are driven by fear. The fear of not being – or no longer being – loved. To me, that's what all those unresolved issues are about. That's why it's so valuable to speak about it while you still can. And of course it's much easier to do so to someone neutral like a hospice care assistant than, say, a wife or daughter. That person can say: 'Tell me about your fear. What does it feel like, what colour is it?' That way, you create a space.

From the wealth of stories told within that space, Christiane zu Salm concludes that it is possible to learn the art of 'inner alignment', which is useful not just in the face of death but even, and especially, when our own death and dying process seem remote. It is, therefore, an art for the present, not the future. 'To make that inner alignment as relevant and meaningful as possible, encounters with the dying are extremely valuable. In that sense, end-of-life care is also the best cure for narcissism.'

If you like, this is a practical exercise in relativization that allows us to see what we *could* do with our lives. One practical approach to this is to write our own obituary. What do we want our legacy to be? During her training as a hospice care assistant, Christiane zu Salm was given fifteen minutes to do just that.

And that central question, 'What do I want my legacy to be?' is monumental. It's existential. That's why the exercise was so challenging, especially against the clock. And afterwards we had to read out our own obituaries to the group! I wanted the ground to swallow me up! How do you do justice to yourself? Was I really a great mother or a successful manager? Or am I hiding my light under a bushel, which is just as vain? And you're not supposed to judge either. How do I go about writing my own obituary without judging?

Later, she asked her patients to write their obituaries, too, and went on to publish them in a book. The range of resulting reflections on a life lived make fascinating reading, partly because they demonstrate the gap between the 'objective' quality of someone's life and their own assessment of it. People who have gone through a lot draw a surprisingly positive picture; others, whose lives have passed largely without incident, conclude that 'life's a bitch, no one ever gave me a chance'. In my view, the *ars moriendi*, or art of dying, isn't the important thing: that's just the starting point for living a good life. As Christiane zu Salm says, the space for action lies before us: it's up to us to take control. Writing your own obituary is one way of understanding this task, and she recommends it to everyone. Such a living obituary is, she says, a 'call to action'. In this case, it is not an obituary for a past life, but one for the life that lies ahead, and one that needs to be 'regularly reviewed and adjusted. The goal must be to eliminate the subjunctives.'

A life that learns to avoid conditionals and what-ifs: that seems to me a good basis for a successful stopping strategy. We must stop thinking about our lives in the subjunctive mood.

And now let me tell you the story of

Hans-Dietrich Reckhaus

Hans-Dietrich Reckhaus has a company that makes insecticides. Together with his brother, he has taken the family firm into its second generation: a solid business with a future. As long as there are annoying and crop-damaging insects, there will be a demand for insecticides. And so business rolls along, until one day Hans-Dietrich designs a new flytrap. Unwilling to splash out on a big advertising campaign for the product, he thinks about hiring an artist to help him come up with a spectacular marketing idea. He turns to the Swiss concept artists Frank and Patrik Riklin, presents his flytrap to them and asks for their suggestions. The artists ask to be given time to think about it. When Reckhaus turns up expectantly at a second meeting, the Riklins tell him they have decided not to work for him: 'Your products are just plain bad. What is a fly worth to you? You should be saving insects, not killing them.'

This response has a lasting impact on Reckhaus. True, he kills insects with his products, but it has never occurred to him up to this point that there could be anything wrong with that. He is cross with the artists, but their brutally frank criticism gets under his skin. Today, he says, 'Those three sentences turned my world upside down.' That was ten years ago. Nowadays, he still produces insecticides, but the insect killer has morphed into an insect saver. How come?

The artists' harsh words continued to prey on Reckhaus's mind. He arranged to meet them again and, instead of pursuing the question of how to market a novel flytrap, he asked them if they could think of a big idea for protecting insects. It is, after all, a commonplace that insects are essential to human survival. They are responsible for pollinating plants, they are an important link in the food chain, especially for birds, and maintain a balance between populations. Without insects, none of this would function, and the fact that insect biomass in Germany has fallen by more than three quarters is, without question, an ecological problem of huge proportions.

And so Reckhaus and the Riklins set to work on two things: first, a campaign to accord flies the attention they deserve from an ecological perspective. And, second, an expanded business model. The campaign is described in detail in Reckhaus's book *Why Every Fly Counts,*[9] and centred on the idea of sending a fly named Erika on a wellness holiday. For any self-respecting German, a decent holiday starts with a flight, and so Erika flew with Lufthansa (naturally on her own seat) from Paderborn to Munich in order to spend a week at the five-star-plus hotel Schloss Elmau (the venue, readers may remember, for the G7 summit during Barack Obama's presidency), before flying home again with Lufthansa. Following her eventual demise, Erika was laid to rest at the University of St Gallen – which has

Fig. 2.4:   Erika in her sarcophagus, University of St Gallen

a first-class art collection – and can be viewed there in a glass sarcophagus.

As you can imagine, the whole campaign attracted a huge amount of attention, but instead of leading to an explosion in sales of the flytrap, it prompted the development of an insect rescue strategy designed to compensate and indeed overcompensate for the insects killed by Reckhaus insecticides. The principle is as follows: for the estimated number of insects killed or likely to be killed in any one case, an area is reserved providing a habitat for a comparably large or larger number of insects. The product is sold under the label 'Insect Respect', which is now emblazoned not just on the packaging of Reckhaus products, but also on that of other insecticide manufacturers who have pledged to take similar compensatory measures. Ten years after its unexpected launch, 'Insect Respect' has become a success story that has turned the entrepreneur's life and world view on its head. Reckhaus says that sales have fallen by 25 per cent and profits by 75 per cent, but he finds his work far more meaningful than before. Because, in essence, it is about giving up an old business model and developing a new one based on a new relationship with nature.

Now every product from his factory bears a label warning *against* its use and providing a wealth of information on insects. It also explains how to avoid using the product entirely and, failing that, how to compensate for the consequences. Furthermore, Reckhaus's company is withdrawing old products and replacing them with 'rescue products' that are beneficial rather than detrimental to insects. Ultimately – and hence the two books he has dedicated to the subject and the many 'Insect Respect' events (Insect Hour, Insect Day, etc.) he has organized – Reckhaus's aim is to develop an entrepreneurial business model that actively contributes to the protection of the biosphere.

That's a hell of a lot in one decade. And although Reckhaus is under no illusion about the worries, frustrations, struggles and losses the psychological and physical conversion of his business model has brought him, he stands as an impressive example of how entrepreneurial activity in a capitalist culture doesn't have to be destructive, even in the case of insecticides. You simply have to stop seeing the profit imperative as the be-all and end-all, and look at it instead as your contribution towards the development of a sustainable economy.

Reckhaus's current ambition is to promote the transformation of business models with a view to achieving a truly sustainable economy; he sees the insect project as one phase in an ongoing process of self-enlightenment. Putting it into practice took a whole lot of stopping.

Stopping, like any other skill, is something that has to be learned.

One day in 2017, I received a call from

Peter Sillem

the managing director of my publishing company, informing me that he would shortly be leaving the company he had spent 30 years working for in order to open a gallery for photographic art. He wondered whether I, as a former gallerist myself (another story!), had any tips. My main piece of advice was that you need a lot of financial staying power to make a living from selling art, and that it's a highly specialized business requiring intensive networking – with the artists on your books as well as with potential customers and, preferably, collectors. On top of that I felt it would be particularly hard to be successful with a photography gallery because a photo doesn't have quite the same brand of uniqueness as a painting or sculpture. In my own time as a gallerist, I had had my share of financial disaster. Although Peter listened to this with interest, I could already tell that nothing would deter him from his plan. He was just about to turn fifty, and felt an urgent desire to move on to pastures new.

I recently talked to him about that decision to stop, and he reflected on how he had felt at the time. Fifty years on the planet, thirty of them with the same employer.

I had to make a decision. Of course, it was also partly to do with the fact that I had followed the institutional path from trainee to freelancer and editor – in short, I'd had what you call a career. By that time I had reached a plateau, especially when I got the job of managing director. I had fulfilled my potential. What next? The thing is, it became increasingly clear to me that I was somehow at the mercy of outside forces in this job, in a way you don't imagine. You expect to have the power to make decisions and assert your will, but in reality you are torn between a thousand different interests and spend a lot of time trying to reconcile them. I overestimated the amount of freedom I would have. That was definitely a factor in my decision to stop. But most of all, it was the realization: I'm fifty now. I have another fifteen or twenty years in which to achieve something. And, funnily enough, the future perfect really does play a huge role in my life. The questions 'How will I have lived, how do I want to have lived, what do I want to have done with my life, which paths do I want to have taken?' That was always a deciding factor for me. My father once coined the term 'biographical wounds' in relation to some decision that needed to be taken. What actions might leave wounds or scars one day – things that might never heal properly?

Peter Sillem can look back on a hugely successful career with the company and, what's more, in a profession that can undoubtedly be described as interesting, meaningful and challenging. But, even here, there comes a point in your life where you find yourself torn between looking back and looking forward, and you need to make a decision. How do I want to have lived? How do I avoid a 'biographical wound' due to a wrong decision or one not taken? Biographical wounds arise from those crossroad situations when you find you've made the wrong choice: not marrying the love of your life, missing the chance of a lifetime, signing the wrong contract. For his part, Peter Sillem took the decision to stop.

His decision comes about almost by chance: while considering whether to take the plunge, he checks out some premises to get an idea of what's involved.

Then I found this place and it all took shape very quickly. I suddenly had a concrete vision of how it might work, and that was the first step towards stopping.

I really only went to find out what such commercial spaces cost. That's how I ended up where we are today – I instantly knew it could be a good fit. And then came the actual process of stopping. I didn't find it hard because I felt I'd reached a point where I needed to draw a line in the sand. That's an important point about stopping. You have to do a lot of thinking and preparation and make a plan for how to stop – an exit strategy for yourself. And then it's really not so difficult.

He is well aware of the economic risk involved, but he is willing to shoulder it: 'It's like the way a lot of people stick around in dysfunctional relationships that they daren't leave. That's probably because the future brings uncertainty. And of course because they are anxious about leaving their familiar environment and its fixed coordinates. However crap the status quo, it's something to hold on to.' Timing is important, too, he adds. He has a picture in his mind of Herbert von Karajan, the famous Austrian conductor of the Nazi era, being heaved into the saddle and looking about a hundred years old. 'If that's the final image you leave behind, I thought, it's not a good look. I always admired Greta Garbo for retiring gracefully at the height of her success. You can't go any higher, so let's call it a day. And that's the whole point: it's about retaining control, refusing to surrender your personal sovereignty. That's what matters to me.'

The important thing, then, is to recognize the point when it would be wrong to continue. Here, too, as with Reinhold Messner and Johannes Heimrath, the risk of banalization is a factor: the time to stop is when you have fully mastered or got to grips with something, otherwise it can end up becoming stale or embarrassing. Stopping is a way of protecting oneself against banality. Greta Garbo was never banal. And another thing we need to learn in order to be able to stop is to be kind to ourselves. After all, you can't expect to perform a new task with the same effortless ease as your old one:

What appealed to me was the chance to switch to a brand new field. It was a clean break from the past. That's the real attraction: recapturing the experience of doing things for the first time. The luxury of allowing yourself to make mistakes.

Because mistakes are inevitable: I'm bound to make some, but I'll be doing it knowingly. And I won't beat myself up about it. I'll take them in my stride and say, right, I can tick that off as a lesson learned. That tolerance towards yourself and your own failures is important.

Stopping is associated with the fear of making mistakes, perhaps even the ultimate mistake of giving up one's familiar, safe existence. In order to stop, therefore, we need to be willing to make mistakes without blaming ourselves. That seems to me an excellent strategy for avoiding the 'if-onlys' that Christiane zu Salm talked about. The best way to avoid disappointments is to be realistic about them. 'History only tastes bitter to those who expected it to be sugar-coated', to quote Chris Marker's film *Sans Soleil*. Or, as Peter Sillem concludes, 'When you only have one life, you have to embrace the crap bits too.'

No wonder the Peter Sillem Gallery has been such a success. And now to

Klaus Wiegandt

Wiegandt is a man who warrants not just one but two biographies. The first is the story of one of Germany's top business managers: in 1976, at the age of thirty-seven, he was appointed general representative of the retail group REWE Leibbrand. Just a year later, Willi Leibbrand made him a co-partner of the family holding. In 1991, he became CEO of the company Asko, which was absorbed into Metro AG in 1996. Wiegandt was one of the co-initiators of the spectacular merger of Asko, Kaufhof and Metro to form Germany's largest retail group. In the space of three years, Wiegandt and colleagues succeeded in boosting the companies' collective annual sales figure of 60 billion DM by a further 40 billion, making Metro the second biggest retail group in the world after Walmart.

But there is a 'but' – and here comes the second story: Wiegandt had a clause written into his contract allowing him to retire from the company at sixty. Which he duly did. And, in a sense, switched sides. Because he then went on to set up the foundation Forum for Responsibility, organizing regular high-level symposiums on the key questions of human survival. Covering subjects from A for alternative energy to W for water, the list of speakers and authors is a *Who's Who* of contemporary scientific journalism – Jared Diamond, Robin Dunbar, Josef Reichholf, Mojib Latif, to name but a few. At the same time, Wiegandt launched his own book series (initially on the state of the planet, then on concrete utopias), funded translations of key international titles, designed handouts for schools and journalists, provided support for young scientists, and initiated a sustainability prize – all in close cooperation with leading institutes and publishers in the field.

Wiegandt's motivation then and now is twofold: an uncompromising belief in enlightenment and an equally uncompromising desire to prevent the world from becoming any worse than necessary. As a dogged campaigner for the transition to economic and social sustainability, he has focused his efforts in recent years chiefly on a project which he calls 'Forests for the World': based on the recognition that the measures agreed in the Paris Climate Accord will kick in too late if at all, he advocates a three-pronged strategy of rainforest protection, renaturation of degenerated forest and large-scale reforestation. He argues that by planting trees, we can absorb more CO_2 and thus buy time to switch to a post-fossil global economy before the 3°, 4° or 5° scenarios predicted by climate scientists become a reality and the window for action narrows. At a cost of around 140 billion dollars a year, that's not too high a price for the survival of civilization. There are 168 million hectares currently available for reforesting, though the cash – as usual – has yet to be stumped up. But the basic principle of curbing climate change by stopping an old-established practice makes obvious sense.

Wiegandt, as a businessman turned sustainability campaigner, probably owes his success in these two apparently very different spheres of action to the same characteristics: a self-effacing sort dedicated to the cause, he is an invariably affable, clear-thinking and impressive man – not to mention, as a former Metro colleague said of him, an excellent strategist who gets things done. Let's hope for all our sakes that the same goes for the tree-planting project. Deforestation has to stop. It's just a question of putting our money where our mouth is.

And finally, we come to

Slicky Baby

For me, 5 April 2016 was the kind of day that Johannes Heimrath would call an 'exemplary day' – one where an incredible amount happened and where everything seemed to fall into place in the most extraordinary way. Looking back, you wonder how so much could be concentrated into twenty-four hours. On that day, I was walking through New Orleans with the artists Corinna and Jochen Hein. On a street corner, we took a taxi because I wanted to visit the Ninth Ward, the district devastated by Hurricane Katrina in August 2005. Now, more than a decade later, there are just over a thousand households left, out of nearly five thousand before the disaster; the remainder were destroyed and never rebuilt. I had heard about a reconstruction project by Graft Architects, a German company based in Braunschweig, which – with the aid of a charity founded by Brad Pitt and a number of other architecture firms offering their services at cost price – was building 150 houses in Ninth Ward. These houses would be affordable for former residents who had lost their own homes, as well as flood-proof and interesting from an architectural point of view. I was keen to see them.

Sean, the taxi driver, was a bit surly at first, asking why on earth we wanted to go the Ninth Ward of all places, so I explained my reasons. He then made us an offer: why not take an all-in tour of New Orleans while we were at it – he had the whole day free and would quote us a fixed price. We agreed, and it turned out to be one of the best suggestions ever, as we got an impromptu crash course on the city into the bargain and, in particular, on the havoc that Katrina had wrought on the district I was so interested in and where, as we learned, Sean himself had lived. He took us to see the foundations of his old house – all that was left in the wake of Katrina. More than ten years on from the catastrophe, the district still looked completely ruined as we made our way past huge empty spaces between solitary and partially decaying buildings. Most of the houses had never been rebuilt – all you could see were the foundation walls, or redundant steps leading up to non-existent front doors. Destroyed schools, impassable roads and still-legible marks on many of the ruined houses from the time of the floods, made to indicate to the evacuation troops the body count within and the number of people missing.

The Graft project was interesting, but more interesting still was this special insight into the United States and its treatment of particularly vulnerable groups. Or, rather, the poor. Because the Lower Ninth Ward – home to the poorest section of the New Orleans population – was almost completely wiped out by Katrina, and there is a theory (voiced, among others, by Spike Lee in his 2006 film *When the Levees Broke*) that the flood waters were diverted to this almost exclusively African-American district in order to protect the city's famous tourist centre from destruction, thereby sacrificing it along with its inhabitants. Whether or not this is true, the consequences were disastrous. Not just the fact that so many people lost their lives: many of the survivors had to leave the city and attempt to build a new life elsewhere. There was no question of returning in the immediate aftermath, and in the end so few did that, by that time, both the social structure and the ethnic composition of the electorate in favour of African-Americans had radically changed. After Katrina, New Orleans had around 100,000 fewer inhabitants, and most of those who left after losing everything had belonged to the African-American population. Katrina has made New Orleans whiter and wealthier. Black Lives Matter clearly didn't hold true here in the Lower Ninth Ward, and we were standing quite literally on the ruins of inequality and injustice, Brad Pitt or no Brad Pitt. Given the radical destruction still apparent a decade on, it was clear that his project, however good, was hardly capable of remedying the damage. As the sun shone down on this scene of devastation, Sean explained everything, showed us everything, introduced us to remaining residents and guided us around. This is what a society looks like where civil protection is inadequate and social inequality high. One where public welfare has low priority and is at best left to the charity of well-meaning donors. Where people who don't have the money to return to their city simply never come back. There were a few restored houses of course, and needless to say there were people making music on their porches – this was New Orleans, after all. The old clichés invariably hold true.

And just when we thought we'd seen it all, we suddenly ran into a funeral – New Orleans style. A band was playing Creole jazz loudly and joyfully, everyone was dancing in the street, people were holding up placards and wearing T-shirts with slogans like 'Hell of a Nigga'.

The deceased was James Hayes, known as Slicky Baby, and the party was in his honour. In New Orleans, funerals are called 'celebration-of-life services', and we – the disaster tourists – had just stumbled upon this one. It certainly was an exuberant send-off. As someone previously accustomed to the European brand of ritualized mourning, I was completely gobsmacked. Here was a very different way of dealing with death – by celebrating life! We can't know what Slicky Baby

Fig. 2.5:   Slicky Baby's funeral: a cool gig for a cool guy

thought of his funeral, but I guess he would have been horrified had his death been marked in any other way, and this way certainly did him justice.

Here, therefore, is a potted obituary of James Hayes, who left behind six children, eleven grandchildren and an army of nieces, nephews and siblings, and was – judging by the mood at the funeral – a regular guy. His friends and relatives don't articulate their grief at the celebration of life, where the emphasis is on the joy of being alive. The mourning is done in written form. His favourite niece, Latrice, writes to him: 'You left without giving us a warning, that wasn't cool.' By all accounts, this was the only thing that wasn't cool about Slicky Baby.

To me, a German completely unknown to him but of a similar age, James Hayes has bequeathed an important insight: there is a way of taking leave of the dead that pays tribute to their past life but at the same time looks forward to a future that is, and will continue to be, full of life, and which should therefore be celebrated.

In my view, this is a variant of the tamed death discussed at the beginning of this book, and that we in the modern age have lost. In that sense, New Orleans is something of an exclave in the modern culture around death and dying. When I remarked once in private that I should like a funeral like Slicky Baby's, I was instantly jumped upon. Not only was this an instance of blackface-style hostile cultural appropriation by a stupid Central European white man: it was also unreasonable to expect those who wanted to mourn me to sing and dance for joy. It just wasn't right.

Oh well, they knew best, it seemed. For my part, though, I think that turning the business of stopping into a celebration of life is the way to go. I can't imagine anything more caring and life affirming in the face of an essentially sad occasion. In fact, it even makes the prospect of my own inevitable death, which I still can't quite warm to, a little pleasanter. Party on, I say!

III

An Obituary to the Rest of My Life

I have learnt a great deal from writing this book so far: from all the interviews, the literature, my spell in the intensive care unit and the review of my own life, to which I have given much thought over the past year – a process which, incidentally, has brought back some remarkably minor details and emotions I remember feeling in moments I'd thought long forgotten.

Like the following episode from my childhood, for instance. When I was about twelve or thirteen, I set my heart on a pair of suede boots. There was no way my mother was going to buy them for me: calf-length boots in the summertime, what an idea! Shoes had to be practical, not decorative. So I had to save up for them myself. One way I could earn a bit of cash was by taking Michael, the neighbour's lad, to his regular training sessions at the primary school gym. I would take him on my bike, with a primitive second saddle screwed to the frame and two footrests on the fork. Absolutely unthinkable in these days of obsessive health and safety. It all went fine for a while, and each time another 50 pfennigs dropped into my piggybank, bringing the boots closer week by week. Until one fateful day when, as always, I rounded the bend into the schoolyard at speed, ready to sail with practised precision into my usual slot in the cycle rack. Except this time I was so busy showing off that I lost my balance and tumbled sideways in slow motion, taking the bike and little Michael with me. Unfortunately, there was another bike in the neighbouring slot. The cleaning lady's. It was mounted on the stand, so that the front part of her wheel was bent to a right-angle under our weight. And as bad luck would have it Mr Bergander, the caretaker, happened to be just a few yards away at the time. Seeing him observe the damage with great interest, I knew instantly that I could kiss goodbye to the boots, and to all my savings. I picked myself and the child up, gave him a pat ('Off you go to school, Michael'), looked at Bergander, then spun my bike around and pedalled for all I was worth. Bergander ran after me – hey, stop, come back, etc. – but I was already out of sight. Still, I knew that if I ever set foot (or tyre) in that schoolyard again, Bergander would lynch me and I would be liable for the damage. Or worse, for absconding from the scene. And the cleaning lady – what should I say to the poor woman whose bike I had crushed – and who would have to pay for the repairs by the sweat of her brow? I had a terribly bad conscience. In desperation, I announced that I was, sadly, unable to take Michael to training any more. Nor could I explain why. I just couldn't do it any longer. Neither the neighbour nor my mother could understand it. And there was nothing I could do to help them. So I said nothing. I spent weeks in silent panic in case the deed came to light and I was forced to atone. But in the end, I got away with it. Not long after, in fact, I even managed to buy the boots. And a jolly fine pair they were, too.

Another moment that springs to mind, from over a decade later: I am in Mexico, on the terrace of one of those back-of-beyond bars. About twenty yards away is an ancient American, the only other guest. Having watched him trying vainly to light a cigar, I go over to him, offer him a light and return to my table, all without a word. A few minutes later the waiter brings me a beer and nods in the direction of the old man. I raise my glass to him.

Another moment, from shortly before: my love for a female companion evaporates in a split second when, nodding towards a young man in front of us on the bus who is evidently undergoing chemotherapy for cancer, she whispers to me: 'You'd think he'd put a hat on at least!'

No idea why such things should come back to me half a century later. But lots of memories like this have popped into my head over the past year – some of them banal, some consisting of no more than a gesture, a look, or a phrase. They seem to form the texture of one's life. I am reminded of Orson Welles's legendary film *Citizen Kane*, whose plot revolves around the search for the meaning of the tycoon Charles Foster Kane's dying word, 'Rosebud'. There, too, the answer to the riddle is utterly mundane: neither a mysterious code word, nor a reference to some secret society or clandestine affair, but merely the brand name of a child's sledge. No more, no less.

It's the small things like this – a concept, a phrase, a touch, a shock, a surprise, a smile, an inexplicable fixation, a passion – that constitute the fabric of our lives, much more so than the conventional stories we tell ourselves and each other about them. Because life courses are not chains of cause and effect but nodes in a web of relationships, and although these nodes are formed for all kinds of reasons and only very rarely by design, they nevertheless determine what we do – or don't do – next. The Swiss writer Max Frisch excelled at showing how we come to believe that our stories *are* our life. But perhaps life and the things that matter in it are made up of very different particles, like the story of Barbara the beer-bearing night nurse, or my story of the mangled bike and the caretaker. That in itself was a tale of guilt and conscience and the seeming impossibility of resolving a conflict. About doing something even though it's wrong. About feeling lonely and unable to speak in a conflict situation. A deep emotional conflict. What impact did it have on the rest of my life? Such things are best left to psychoanalysts; what we can say, however, is that the important things are not the ones we automatically think of. They are associated with deep-seated emotions, where causes and effects are unrelated.

My obituary to the rest of my life would have to start from the point already discussed in various contexts in this book: the experience of being overwhelmed by fear and 'what-ifs'; the need to quit old routines and habits; the decision to deviate from the plan; the gamble of life itself. And, finally, the moment when something you have explored, grasped and mastered to perfection suddenly becomes banal.

My obituary starts from the age of sixty-two. While Germany braces itself for a further COVID wave, I am sojourning on an island, looking out over the ocean. And happy to go on doing so. Because if my lucky escape from death's clutches has taught me anything, it's the importance of laziness. As someone who has risen from so-called humble circumstances, I was driven for decades by two things: ambition and the fear of poverty. (A ludicrous fear on the face of it but something that lies well below the level of rational consciousness – a kind of learned, occupational anxiety, like a mental equivalent to a carpenter's overdeveloped thumb or a jockey's bow legs.)

This combination of ambition and anxiety leads in turn to overwork, stress and a chronic fear of not doing enough. And hence to a tendency to juggle too many things – too many projects at once, too many engagements, too many commitments, both real and perceived. And of course, quite apart from all that, to an excessive vanity that has to be constantly fed. Personal best: four lectures in three cities in two days. And all the while preaching about the need to pursue a simpler lifestyle, pause for breath and make do with less. Ha, ha. The other grim irony was that my heart attack didn't come at a time of high anxiety. Like when your train breaks down, your appointment looks doomed, you spend ages trying to persuade railway officials to open the doors, you organize a taxi, you arrive at the venue completely stressed out and try to relax in the evening by drinking so much that you're fit for nothing the next day – that sort of thing. No, it came during what was – thanks to the first COVID lockdown – the most relaxed period I can remember since childhood. If it had hit me on a station platform, it would have been less of a surprise.

As far as rest and relaxation goes, I'd get twitchy after a week's holiday (or, at the most, nine days); there was always too much to do. Now I've been living on my island for nearly four months like some castaway, and I am amazed at how much practice and willpower it takes to simply let go. True, I'm writing a book and doing a good few Zoom conferences, but I have plenty of time on my hands, and my Protestant work ethic is constantly telling me I really ought to be doing something useful instead of going to the beach again. In other words, it's not just the act of stopping that has to be learnt but the refusal to consider every available unit of time in terms of its utility value. A starry sky like this is beautiful, even though you can't do anything with it except look at it. And so I have prescribed myself a time-wasting programme which is already working so well that I get irritated when anything distracts me from my new beach-going and swimming ritual. Progress indeed.

I have learnt to prefer slothing over beavering – at least occasionally. If I climb a mountain, I am more interested in stopping, turning round and looking at the valley below than in seeing how fast I can get to the top. Another milestone. And because I have virtually no social life – amazingly, the brief exchanges when buying a paper, my language courses, and Zooms with faraway people are all I need – I'll even watch a couple of films in the evening, though I hardly dare say it. But it's rather enjoyable now and again and does no one any harm, not even me.

As far as my obituary to myself goes, my plan for the rest of my life is to continue practising this exercise in alternative time use and stargazing, and to get better at it. It's too late to make up for the omissions of a lifetime, but I can still learn to cultivate a more conscious, positive attitude to time, and to free both it and myself from the constraints of utility.

I want my obituary to say:
He was a good time waster

A few years ago, the writer Karoline Walter did a wonderful piece for our sustainability platform FUTURZWEI about one of her flatmates – a bone-idle sort who dodged chores wherever he could and spent most of his time doing nothing. Analysing his behaviour from a sustainability perspective, however, she found that – thanks to his spectacular laziness – this guy used far fewer resources than his ecologically zealous contemporaries. He consumed less simply because he did less. This is an instructive and practical counter-model to modernity's constant pursuit of boundlessness. Because even a good eco-warrior lives by the rule of optimization and is forever having to justify their actions to themselves: why they made this or that journey by car or even by plane, whether they bought the most ethical veg from the most ethical source, or whether they wrapped the baby in enough fabric nappies so that it doesn't end up carrying a full ecological backpack. Here, too, the universal paradigm is one of optimization, not stopping: things must get better, not worse.

I know I am treading a fine line here, as I am naturally all for people being aware of the resources they use and consume, but at the same time I feel that, sadly, we often have the right answers to the wrong questions. After all, we would already manage our resources much better if only we weren't constantly subject to the mania of optimization – even when that mania is in a good cause.

Many years ago, the late philosopher Peter Heintel founded a 'Society for the Deceleration of Time', whose members

– in their heyday – would organize excursions to places such as famous ski World Cup venues, where they would comb the slopes for the missing tenths of seconds 'lost' by the ski champions. Because that's what it all comes down to in such highly professionalized sports: the thousandths, hundredths and tenths of a second a competitor loses over the course and which stand between them and victory. And because there can only ever be one winner, there must be a hell of a lot of seconds for the Society's members to find after any World Cup. If you're now wondering whether their mission was successful, then you are very far from an answer.

Then there is the conceptual artist Nikolaus Huhn, the inventor of the 'Walking Ears'. In 2013, Huhn spent two months pushing a cart with giant ears through the towns, cities and districts of Thuringia for 745 miles, listening to people as he went. Wherever he ended up, he organized discussion evenings, asking questions such as: What do you live on? What do you heat with? Is there a well here? Sometimes, people would walk part of the way with him the next day in order to continue the discussion, and he would make a note of their

Fig. 3.1:   The Walking Ears: a listening project

conversations. He too is interested in time: 'I am from a generation for whom it has been five minutes to midnight for 30 years. This burning desire to be a witness to the end of the world is just another form of vanity. It's already well past five minutes to midnight. It's half past three, we're drinking coffee, everything's fine.'

It is curious how such simple sentences manage to bring about such a disorientating change of perspective. Huhn simply posits a different reality, which serves to open up a hitherto unexplored cognitive space. His art lies not in embellishing, supplementing and augmenting the familiar, but merely evaluating it anew. And the results are of course not only discombobulating but sometimes very funny too.

Heintel and Huhn, masters of non-optimization.

I want my obituary to say:
He learnt to resist optimization

I don't think I'll nail that one entirely, but that's OK.

'What are you working on?', Mr K. was asked. Mr K. replied: 'I'm having a hard time, I'm preparing my next mistake.' This story by Bertolt Brecht is called 'Hardships of the Best'. And rightly so. After all, only the best know that mistakes need to be well prepared. Only the best know that mistakes and errors are a good thing if you know how to apply them. They are no trifling matter: on the contrary, you have to work at them. How wasteful is the desire to avoid mistakes and errors; what nonsense to seek to prevent people – students, for instance – from making them. We learn nothing from the mistakes of others. An uncompromisingly positivist determination to do everything right never ventures beyond the perceived limits of possibility. The architect Wolfgang Rossbauer explained this phenomenon to me very memorably with reference to Gothic cathedrals:

The Gothic cathedrals had to collapse. A computer simulation isn't nearly as effective. We try to simulate collapse, but there is no pain involved, so it's not really the same experience. I'm a bit nostalgic for that time. Today, we only see the cathedrals that remained standing. Not the ones that failed. Pain is an inevitable part of the artistic process. And if I don't embrace that pain, I won't get the right results.

Indeed, it wasn't uncommon for those soaring Gothic cathedrals to collapse in dramatic fashion due to the attempt to build ever higher naves and vaults. Beauvais Cathedral in northern France, for example, had a 48.5-metre-high transept and collapsed shortly after completion of the first construction phase in 1284; an improved version was then built in a process lasting several decades. The same fate subsequently befell the spire which, at 153 metres, was the tallest structure at the time (we're talking 1573 by now, mind you – that's how long things lasted in the days before sustainability was invented): it collapsed spectacularly, causing considerable damage to the rest of the church. The pain Rossbauer was talking about must have been enormous, given the huge amount of work that went into it over centuries, but it did at least prove a point: there is a limit to how high you can go. By contrast, a computer simulation doesn't hurt, which is perhaps more dangerous in the medium term than a painful failure that teaches us an important lesson.

Moreover, mistakes are only mistakes if they have con-sequences. Take Chernobyl, for instance: it wasn't just that the safety test went wrong (which would barely have raised an eyebrow), but the fact that it led to the biggest nuclear disaster in history. Astonishingly, the concept of error seems to attract little scientific interest, even though it has shaped human history since Adam took a bite of the apple, or at least since a wooden horse full of Greek soldiers entered the city of Troy. One exception – and a very witty one, as it happens – is

Fig. 3.2:   Collapsed cathedral: learning the art of failure

Sigmund Freud's *Psychopathology of Everyday Life*. Mistakes are not only revealing when the father of the bride accidentally refers to his 'swine-in-law' instead of his 'son-in-law', however, but can also highlight systemic failures: when design flaws are covered up by software, for example, as in the case of the Boeing 737 Max or the diesel emissions scandal, or – as in the case of the German payment processor Wirecard – when they point to a whole series of criminal activities. But isn't it more important than ever, when chains of activity and dependency are growing increasingly long and opaque, to view mistakes in a whole new light: not as nuisances to be avoided and concealed but as clues to systemic failures whose consequences will be all the more serious the longer they go uncorrected?

Some time ago, the organizational psychologists Karl Weick and Kathleen Sutcliffe wrote the aptly titled book *Managing the Unexpected*.[1] In it, they analysed so-called high-reliability organizations – institutions in which errors can have not just inconvenient but catastrophic consequences. Examples are nuclear power stations, aircraft carriers, fire services, hostage negotiation teams, civil protection systems and so on. The work of such organizations is aimed primarily at *preventing* certain events from occurring, which is why much of what is deemed valuable in other organizations is actually problematic in their case: any kind of routine, for example, is a bad thing because it undermines a person's sensitivity to impending problems. Experience leads to a premature assumption that any given event is something that has happened before, and should therefore be regarded and treated in the usual way – a frequently fatal mistake. Thus experience can become a trap when something looks familiar but is actually a completely different ball game: this is how both the *Challenger* disaster and the Chernobyl nuclear meltdown came about.

Planning procedures, too, are based on existing data and ways of doing things, which is why they often fall fatally short of the actual requirements and challenges that would need to be addressed in order to manage a new or unanticipated problem. When it comes to dealing with the unexpected, the key is to develop an instinct for when something looks likely to happen that would instantly overwhelm the routine systems in place; if anything, therefore, one should be mistrustful of experience and consider each phenomenon with fresh eyes. That message really hits home after a critical life event like my illness, when it would indeed have been very stupid to carry on as before. The fact that things have been 'all right up to now' is not a reliable guide to future action.

I'm not just talking about the individual context, however. As societies become increasingly vulnerable – due to environmental stress and over-long dependency chains – we need a new approach to the concept of error. It's time to call off the tedious search for a culprit whenever *x* or *y* happens. To learn once and for all that mistakes are constructive, but – crucially – only if they are not covered up or blamed on someone else. It's time to stop trusting in crystal-clear and hard-and-fast decisions by so-called decision makers – they are no longer any use (if they ever were) once the situation has changed. All they do, sadly, is to perpetuate the status quo.

One approach that helps us to refrain from instantly assigning everything that meets the eye to the categories of the known and familiar is, according to Weick and Sutcliffe, that of mindfulness. All this means is the practice of constantly reviewing and revising our expectations, together with a heightened awareness of possible errors and irregularities – in short, a continuous learning process within an ever-changing environment. In this context, mistakes are not regarded as bad but as highly important sources of information on possible scenarios. While the normal tendency is to avoid mistakes and, when they happen, to try and hush them up, in this case a mistake is seen as something very valuable: thus employees who identify errors in high-reliability organizations are not harassed but honoured.

According to Weick and Sutcliffe, mindfulness diverts the attention from the expected to the irrelevant, from the confirming to the disconfirming, from the pleasant to the unpleasant, from the explicit to the implicit, from the consistent to the inconsistent. And this reversal of perspective can be triggered by the very phenomenon of error that is so misread in our contemporary culture.

A culture in which everyone claims to be doing everything right can only be one of two things: deeply divided or completely anaesthetized. Both are unproductive – especially when the biggest challenge of the twenty-first century is to build our economic metabolism on a new, non-destructive economic system, and no one knows how to do it. As noted earlier, it is a fantasy of the growth-based economy that the policy of so-called decarbonization will solve our problems: if the size of our metabolism continues to increase, so will the destruction, with or without CO_2. The trouble is, nobody knows how to build a naturally conflict-free economy and society that will see us through the twenty-first century. To acquire that knowledge will take a collective learning process that can best be advanced by learning from our mistakes. The driverless car is a mistake because it perpetuates individual transport. The digitalization of infrastructures is a mistake because it increases their vulnerability. The externalization of costs is a mistake because it makes others pay for the destruction from which we profit. The drive for cost efficiency is a mistake because it hinders resilience. The homogenization of culture is a mistake because it destroys society's greatest productive force: diversity.

Mistakes are not a reason to attack each other or apportion blame but an opportunity to do things better. To paraphrase Bertolt Brecht, A doesn't necessarily lead to B but perhaps to the recognition that A was wrong. And, having once discovered this, to the further recognition that – like Peter Sillem – we should learn to be kind to ourselves.

I want my obituary to say: He always tried to make useful mistakes

Reinhold Messner, Johannes Heimrath and Peter Sillem all subscribed to the maxim – based on personal experience – that the time to quit is when you have mastered something to perfection. Carrying on past that point only banalizes it. Looking back on my life, I can't say that there are many things I have mastered to perfection. The sad truth is that I'm not good at anything much, except perhaps speaking and writing and generally being a smartass. No, I had other reasons for quitting. I gave up a promising career as a journalist in my mid-twenties because my editor told me – at least, that's how I interpreted it then – that I didn't have the right attitude for the job. 'Mr Welzer, you confuse journalism with superficiality!' Although I was very hurt at the time, the said editor – Jochen Döring, then head of Science and Technology at the broadcasting company NDR – was, alas, quite right. I guess I was too busy flashing my mic and tape recorder around and collecting soundbites instead of constructing well-researched articles. Yet I did genuinely want to be a journalist, and I was very proud of having made it into radio at a time when job prospects for arts graduates were pretty grim. Now I had to think again.

All right then, I thought, why not do a PhD – it might be interesting and will improve your chances on the job market. And by an incredible stroke of luck I ended up studying under the psychologist Ali Wacker, an acknowledged expert on unemployment research who set me on a gradual path to an academic career. Although I already had an MA, it was from him that I really learnt the art of scholarship. For that I am grateful to him to this day because he helped me improve, thanks – among other things – to constant criticism. The first time I was invited to publish a joint essay with him, I handed him with some trepidation the passages I had sweated over, and awaited his verdict with bated breath. They were, he announced without further elaboration, 'no good'. And so I started again from scratch until they were eventually pronounced 'good'. Another academic giant I greatly admired was Raul Hilberg, the pre-eminent scholar of the Holocaust. He once confessed to me on a walk that he was afraid of sometimes forgetting details in his lectures, which were brilliant and always delivered completely from memory. He supposed he was getting old. For Hilberg, 'details' meant sentences like: 'When Senior Group Leader So-and-So entered office 117 on the morning of 13 April 1943 . . .' – as I say, entirely without notes. 'Oh, Mr Hilberg', I replied, 'that's nothing to do with age, I'm like that already.' At this, Hilberg gave me a perplexed look and opined: 'Then you don't have the skill!'

OK, I thought, we'll see about that. And eventually I learnt to deliver my lectures from memory – something that still gives me a buzz, and which offers an advantage that no PowerPoint karaoke singer ever gets to enjoy. When you speak without notes, you interact with your audience, and that's a wonderful

Fig. 3.3:   Hilberg: master of flattery

way of guiding you through your own thoughts and helping
you to express them in a manner that gives the whole thing
coherence, suspense and – hopefully – substance. The writer
Heinrich von Kleist described this very effect in his essay 'On
the Gradual Construction of Thoughts during Speech'. Another
benefit is that it stops you boring yourself to tears and instead
allows you to try out, elaborate or discover new arguments as

you go. It is an utter mystery to me how colleagues manage to deliver the same lecture over and over without feeling like their own ventriloquist's dummy.

Anyway, to return to my point, brutal criticism was my greatest friend, and I still enjoy a good panning as long as it's intelligently done. (I realize that some fellow writers will be shuddering as they read this: each to his own!) Good criticism is the opposite of banal: it's both a great honour and a learning exercise. Indeed, learning something new is never banal, and I have always moved on to a new research topic as soon as I felt I had answered an academic question, which was also invariably a personal one for me.

I would never have dreamt of devoting the rest of my life to Holocaust and perpetrator studies once I had (in my view) understood what prompts 'perfectly normal' people to participate in mass murder and acts of extreme violence. For I had not only (by my lights) answered this question but also learnt that there are certain potentials that are developed or suppressed depending on the circumstances. What matters is the situation in which those potentials develop; a person's biographical baggage is of secondary importance. This is why people do things they would never have believed themselves capable of. This insight was instrumental in enabling me, after years of unedifying research into murder and homicide, to move on to the question of how to facilitate positive, proactive behaviour. And so on and so forth. Long story short, it was important to me to resist the temptation of banality and cultivate the kind of mental alertness that had so impressed me in my role models.

I believe that went a long way towards helping me quit my successive careers, although, as mentioned, I was in most cases far from achieving perfect mastery of them. I have been a journalist (so-so), a university lecturer (quite good), a gallerist (unsuccessful), a singer in a band (dead loss), an author (quite good), a founder and co-founder of institutions (average) and a researcher in the fields of perpetrator studies (quite good), memory (quite good) and transformation (what can I say?). In short, I have never shone at anything but have always tried to think things through radically and act accordingly wherever possible. My friend and former colleague Gerd Weiberg once described me as 'always radical, never consistent' (something Walter Benjamin once wrote about himself): praise indeed.

I want my obituary to say:
He was nutty, frivolous, interesting, stimulating,
arrogant, annoying, illuminating, unjust –
but never banal

Apropos of that Benjamin quote, it is my suspicion that the demand for consistency – by contradicting the ideal of freedom and autonomy – makes people prisoners of their own minds. In her book *The Origins of Totalitarianism*, Hannah Arendt argued that logical consistency is one of the root causes of the totalitarian mindset, something she illustrates with reference to the conspiracy theory of a Jewish quest for world domination:

> The point was that the Nazis acted as though the world were dominated by the Jews and needed a counter-conspiracy to define itself. Racism for them was no longer a debatable theory of dubious scientific value, but was being realized every day in the functional hierarchy of a political organization in whose framework it would have been very 'unrealistic' to question it.[2]

This assessment mirrors a remark by Joseph Goebbels, who notes in his diary entry for 20 August 1941, 'One need only imagine what the Jews would do to us, if they had the power to do so – as we have the power to do.'[3]

In other words, you start with a theory, organize the world accordingly and regard every element of reality as confirmation

Fig. 3.4:   Moscow: the only subway in the world

of your theory. And once the process of apparent logical consistency is put into practice, reality begins to be organized in line with the theory: 'The assertion that the Moscow subway is the only one in the world is a lie only so long as the Bolsheviks have not the power to destroy all the others.'[4] Nowadays, this same principle is known as path dependency, meaning, on one hand, that certain actions have consequences that leave no alternatives, but also that the actual question or problem that prompted the action in the first place has been forgotten.

At an individual level, this makes people more likely to act according to the maxim 'in for a penny, in for a pound' than to take back their original penny. Consequently, they often become trapped by constraints of their own making, forgetting that they ever had an origin or cause, and that they are by no means objectively inevitable. Unravelling such constraints is precisely what psychotherapists do, and the reason why this is often far from easy is that, first, they are not perceived as constraints ('Just because you're paranoid doesn't mean they aren't after you'), and second, they provide orientation. This was what Peter Sillem meant when he talked about the human tendency to cling to dysfunctional relationships: better the devil you know.

Although, like anyone else, I have my share of such constraints (such as the fear of poverty), I have always tried – sometimes even successfully – to ignore rather than pander to them. Take the economically absurd idea of opening a gallery, for example – a project diametrically opposed to my need for security. Add to that the fact that I am the world's worst salesman and come across as far too arrogant to attract many clients. Those who wished nevertheless to collect works by the artists I presented either had to put up with this personality defect or purchase them elsewhere, from a friendlier gallery. In short, the whole thing was a bit of a fiasco financially, but I funded that fiasco for ten years because it gave me something very different: access to a world whose values and functions were the very opposite of those of academia. I met some really interesting people, travelled widely and learnt a huge amount while enjoying myself along the way. I could say it was worth the money, but to do so would be once again to evaluate the quality of this phase of my life in monetary terms: on the contrary, I mean it was a great time that has enriched my life to this day.

As all this goes to show, it is madness to make the only life we have a slave to consistency and not allow ourselves to deviate from our self-chosen path. That doesn't mean we shouldn't practise to the full the things we will one day – thankfully – leave behind. Indeed, perhaps the knowledge that we can stop at any time enables us to indulge in them with even greater intensity and persistence. What is really irksome is when people cling unshakeably to something they once learnt and decided to adopt as their credo. It might have felt right at the time and made sense in that particular context, but there comes a point when such a belief can prevent you from thinking ahead and getting on with your life, and from then on it becomes something you simply circle around, unable to find a way out. The philosopher Odo Marquard hit the nail on the head when he said, 'Everyone needs a dose of Adorno in their lives, like a dose of measles.' It's a good thing to have engaged with and understood – almost to the point of inhaling – Adorno's thinking, but it would be fatal to get bogged down in it. Those who do so are merely disciples who judge themselves and their world according to what Adorno would have said. They can get by on that if they're lucky, but it is not an attractive personality trait.

I want my obituary to say:
He was always radical, yet always willing to
be inconsistent

Talking of classic theories and ideas that everyone needs to have had – like a dose of measles – to immunize them against the seductions of hermetic constructs, there are of course many more examples I could name. In my days as a sociology student, 'structures' and 'systems' were all the rage. They could be used to explain all sorts of things, and they had the added advantage of enabling you to see through things you would never understand by naively observing human behaviour. No, human beings were the objects – you could almost say pawns – of prevailing capitalist, bureaucratic, gender-specific and various other structures, and in the eyes of any good system theorist there were no people in the world at all, only the systems they blindly served.

Society, then, was understood as a web consisting of all kinds of things – but not people. They were nowhere to be seen, either among, behind or beneath all these structures, and anyone who looked for them instantly betrayed themselves as academically inferior.

Thinking in systems and structures is very attractive because it allows us to observe the world and the people in it like a behavioural scientist observing rats in a maze. And just as a behavioural scientist never joins the rats in the maze, so the habit of thinking in systems and structures has the inestimable advantage of allowing one to keep out of it all, yet at the same time to be more knowledgeable than everyone else. Those who go through their lives like this never waste much time on the real world, its contradictions, and their own small part in the greater whole, but stand above it. What's more, they enjoy the priceless personal advantage of always being right. That's why certain theories appeal so much to simpler minds: if you jump on the psychoanalysis bandwagon, for instance, you can always fend off critical objections with the diagnosis: 'You would say that, wouldn't you: classic defensive behaviour!'

In my case, my sojourn in the 'ice desert of abstraction' was, fortunately, followed by a resurgence of interest in the role of human beings in reality, and in particular how they perceive their world, how they interpret those perceptions and what conclusions they draw from their interpretations. After all, you can only find out why people perform certain actions by trying to see the reality as they saw it at the time. Looking at things from this angle, you suddenly begin to understand why people choose – and not uncommonly either – to act in a way that, viewed objectively, seems to makes no sense or even to go against their own interests.

Such behaviour continues to provoke widespread bafflement to this day: among political journalists who never cease to wonder at Trump voters, for example, or commentators mystified by the 'irrational' behaviour of people who choose to buy giant SUVs despite being fully aware of the climate crisis. Seen through the eyes of the individuals concerned, however, both phenomena are easy to understand: as an extremely gifted populist politician with a firm grasp of the media, Trump has succeeded in building a certain community. And for his supporters, membership of a community welded together by a common belief is something highly valuable and attractive that doesn't even need to have any political content. Trumpism provides a home for the politically homeless, however much it may contradict their 'objective interests'. It's really quite simple. And the case of the SUV driver is no more mysterious: as noted earlier, they may have concluded from all the alarming publicity about the climate situation that, with such a grim future in prospect, it's best to squeeze as much out of the present as humanly possible. After all, who knows how long before such monstrosities are banished from our roads?

If we only look at structures and systems, we will systematically overlook the fact that, regardless of inherent constraints and 'objective' reality, it is also invariably true that the actions of individuals can be the very thing that causes events to take a different turn. Again, these are people who do not act in their 'objective interests' or according to criteria of 'individual net benefit maximization' and whose behaviour cannot be explained by either systems or structural theory. They just act. Such people are evidently convinced that it is up to them to take action, and that it makes a difference whether they do or do not. A case in point are those who suddenly show a remarkable dedication to a cause which continues to grow over their lifetime.

Many years ago, we conducted a study on the behaviour of people who helped and rescued persecuted individuals under the Nazis, and one of the most astonishing findings was that many of those who became helpers and rescuers weren't born with altruistic personalities, but rather found themselves by chance in a situation where they felt duty-bound to help – people with summerhouses that could be used as hiding places, for instance, or doctors who could treat sick children. Quite often, such people went on to become full-time volunteers: sometimes, having agreed at first reluctantly to a request for help ('All right, just this once!'), they became veritable experts after a couple of months, hiding multiple victims and discovering organizational talents they didn't know they had. This was also, incidentally, the experience of countless volunteers in the wake of the so-called refugee crisis in the late summer of 2015: they suddenly discovered other skills outside their existing roles, such as organizing and coordinating.

What can we conclude from this? Two things: first, that any step you take leads you in a particular direction. Taking the same step each time increases the likelihood that you will continue in the same direction; taking an unfamiliar one increases the likelihood that you will continue along the new path. Second, taking that unfamiliar step makes you see yourself in a new light: you discover what else you can do, how to *overcome* your own fears and inhibitions, and how people behave towards you *in this particular situation.*

Since reaching this understanding, I have come to regard the business of structures and systems as an appealing myth that absolves us of our own responsibility and ultimately leads to the excuse that it makes no difference whether or not you vote, fly on holiday, drive a car, or take an interest in others. It's all just a drop in the ocean – of capitalism, that is, or the Great Injustice, or the General Deception.

But this is simply not true. There are individuals like the early German communist and feminist pioneer Clara Zetkin, who taught the Social Democrats that a workers' movement without a women's movement was only half the battle. Or like the (non-Jewish) joiner Georg Elser, who attempted to assassinate Hitler while millions of fellow non-Jewish Germans followed the Führer unconditionally. Or like the typesetter Lutz Beisel, who arranged for injured children in the Vietnam War to be treated in German hospitals. This example is particularly relevant because there were hundreds of thousands of others in the same situation at the same time who witnessed what was happening to children in faraway Asia on their television screens, and many of them must have shared the same acute sense of outrage, anger and grief. But only Lutz Beisel found it so intolerable that he – a conscientious objector – approached

the Bundeswehr and, after much conflict and even greater persistence, finally succeeded in getting military supply planes to
bring injured children to Germany by return flight. This was,
incidentally, the birth of the Swiss children's aid charity Terre
des Hommes, to which 15 million children owe their lives and
health to date.

Compassion costs nothing, but it's no use unless followed up
with action. It takes proactive engagement to change things. I
could reel off a list of people who, not content with looking on,
sympathizing, arguing and offering wisdom, wanted to make a
difference and did so. It ranges from the retired cycle mechanic
who teaches refugees to repair bikes, to the woman on ben-
efits who makes fabulous cushions from fabric remnants for
children in cancer wards, right through to wealthy individuals
who found charities in order to do something useful with their
money.

We at FUTURZWEI collect a host of stories about people
who make a difference through their actions, and without
them all the systems and structures would be unrecognizable.
Indeed, I hope with some justification to make a difference
through my books and sometimes through lectures, as I often
get letters or emails from people telling me what they have
achieved after being inspired and motivated – by my book
Thinking for Yourself, for example – to branch out into something new. And sometimes I read them and think: wow, you're
putting me to shame! They are all making a difference, and it
makes me very proud to think that I was able to give them that
last little push.

I want my obituary to say:
He made a difference

When it comes to making a difference, incidentally, it is totally
irrelevant how big or small that difference is. The important

thing is not to punch below your weight. In a free society, especially one as rich as Germany, everyone has the power to act. The degree of that power varies according to social situation, state of health, age, gender and personal characteristics, but hardly anyone has none at all. As we saw in our discussion of structures and systems, we are practised at making that power look less than it really is. 'There's nothing you can do' is the usual refrain – but those who make that claim have never put it to the test.

Since my episode in intensive care, I know what it means when people are convinced that there is *always* something you can do. And the dedication of hospital staff during the COVID crisis has also shown me how our society has failed to equip these people – who have worked themselves to the bone – with the powers that a modern and resilient health system really needs. I can fully understand why the people who have been holding things together are quitting their jobs in frustration and leaving the profession – they are treated too shabbily by the public sector.

People can only go on chipping away at the barriers and obstacles to active participation for so long. And that is why a forgotten task of politics in a democracy is to increase people's scope for action so that they feel empowered – at their own initiative and risk – to tackle abuses or implement ideas that further the common good. We saw this during the COVID crisis, too, when arrogant politicians and administrators unwilling to assume responsibility themselves stood in the way of proven solutions, leading not only to frustration but to more deaths than necessary.

Citizens of an open society should see their role as an enabling one, regardless of their social position. I was very lucky in that respect – partly, it has to be said, thanks to the failure of my career in journalism and my entry into the university system. Because the great privilege of being a lecturer also brings with it a fantastic enabling opportunity: that of inspiring

people to think for themselves, not to be satisfied with the easy
option, and to take pleasure in the discovery that they have
more talents than they thought. The greatest compliment I
have ever received came from a student I had never seen before
and who hadn't attended any of my lectures or seminars. He
wanted me to set him an exam, which I found very odd. When
I asked him why me, when we didn't even know each other, he
replied, 'I've heard that you sometimes fail people.'

It was, he said, a disgrace that no one else was challenging him – in other words, that it didn't matter whether his
work was good or bad. Yet the whole point of a university,
as I understand it, is that this does indeed matter very much.
And anyone fortunate enough to exercise such a privileged
occupation should use it to open up spaces to students that
they would otherwise struggle to access. As such, it is hor-
rifying that, because of a false self-conception on the part of
lecturers as well as many university executives, we leave young
people to stew in their own juices and fail to offer them any
resistance to get worked up and angry about. Nothing to pique
their narcissism, no challenges to make them question their
own judgement.

I'm not talking about discipline or similarly pointless
approaches but the opening up of possibilities that would otherwise remain closed. And that opening-up process happens
when there are no hierarchies. As a student, I didn't learn
research methodologies (or indeed programming) at university
but as an assistant at a research company where the head of
survey research, Lothar Birk, taught me an enormous amount.
It was obvious that he was head of the department, but only
from his expertise, not from any boss-like behaviour. We once
stopped speaking to each other for a whole week following an
argument – no easy feat when you share an office and need
to interact every now and again. Consequently, all necessary
communications were conducted via colleagues: 'Please ask
Lothar . . .', 'Tell Harald . . .' and so on. I mean: I was the student

assistant, at the very bottom of the hierarchical food chain, and Lothar Birk the much older, more competent and experienced head of department. He could easily have thrown me out, for example, but no, he conducted the quarrel with this young upstart on equal terms and in all its delightful absurdity. The anti-hierarchical approach to work organization that Lothar demonstrated back then, and his way of showing appreciation through his actions, was a great example to me. I have always tried in all my own research projects as well as in organizations such as FUTURZWEI to avoid letting hierarchies and controls creep in, as people work best when they are left to develop their own potential, rather than being spoonfed or bullied. We have no fixed working hours or holidays, no timesheets or other such nonsense. Because a small, flexible, dedicated organization like FUTURZWEI stands or falls by the commitment of all its staff, whether professors, students, eco-volunteers or interns. Nor is there any management board preventing them from taking initiatives as they see fit. This is not only a very efficient system in that no time or money are wasted on controlling, but it is also a very agreeable one, thanks to the sheer pleasure of working together towards a shared goal.

I want my obituary to say:
He created space for people to act

Many people in so-called positions of responsibility restrict people's freedom to act. I can think of a few directors of public broadcasting companies for a start who are guilty of this. Since their obligation is to society rather than to any shareholders, there is nothing to stop them making good programmes. They simply need to work on the assumption that their audience consists of thinking people who are interested in things, including more demanding content. By that I mean quality films, music, features, interviews, research, news reporting and comment.

As I say, they don't need to push up their ratings in order to attract as much advertising as possible and maximize their income. They have a statutory obligation which includes education. It is one of the unsolved mysteries of humankind why a responsible person with such a mandate can abolish culture programmes, declare literary criticism superfluous, deem all interviews lasting more than seven minutes too long – in short, deprive their fee-paying public of everything they are supposed to provide. Instead, they are obsessed with ratings, which they hope to boost with cheap entertainment – comedies, quizzes and talk shows whose aim seems to be to rule out any possibility of an interesting discussion. These generally set people with diametrically opposed views against each other so as to guarantee a heated debate. Brilliant. I have never understood what the value of a heated debate is supposed to be, apart from playing to the gallery (one good thing about COVID was the fact that talk shows took place without a studio audience, so the guests were less motivated by the desire for cheap applause). With a staged debate, everyone concerned comes out less enlightened than when they went in. With a genuine discussion in which two or more people attempt to agree on something, the opposite is the case. A good discussion is more than the sum of the participants' ideas: rather, it sparks off new ideas they would never have thought of independently. And people enjoy listening to such exchanges – that's why Hannah Arendt's discussion with the political commentator Günther Gaus from the early days of German television is still a hit on YouTube, and that's why the journalist Tilo Jung's interviews on his political web show *Jung & Naiv* ('Young and Naive') with people like Noam Chomsky, the former CDU leader Annegret Kramp-Karrenbauer or the philosopher Richard David Precht attract hundreds of thousands of viewers. Ah, but then such interviews last a minimum of ninety minutes, and sometimes even two hours. Public broadcasting directors, take note! Try and find out why people watch and comment on this type of content. No, let me tell you: because no one likes being treated like a moron. No one. Really.

Indeed – and this brings me to my main point – simply taking people and events in general seriously would be a good start. That goes for media chiefs and also of course for actors in politics, NGOs and event agencies. Listening to the same predictable reactions from all sides to every political development in Germany really grates on me. When a supply chain act is passed that constitutes a genuine game changer in terms of corporate responsibility but is in fact only a first step, it is immediately followed by the trade associations' tedious lament that German businesses will be put at a competitive disadvantage. Etc. Meanwhile, the NGOs complain that the new law doesn't go nearly far enough and falls short of human rights laws. Etc. The same thing happens when a member of a political party puts forward an important proposal or idea which is then instantly and 'decisively' rejected as inadequate, wrong, misleading, etc., as if 'decisiveness' were a virtue in itself. Ditto when politicians have to argue in public for things they know are perfectly idiotic and present them with a smile as if they were the result of a long and carefully considered analysis. The speaker invariably professes to be 'firmly convinced' (plain 'convinced', it seems, is not enough). A case in point was Chancellery chief of staff (and medical doctor) Helge Braun's defence of what were clearly half-baked COVID decisions at the end of February 2021. He could have refused to approve the easing of restrictions from a medical point of view and resigned from his post: after all, those wrong decisions cost human lives. Instead, he made a 'firmly convinced' fool of himself. To me, this shows a lack of seriousness, and I wish to claim the right to treat things with the seriousness they truly deserve.

That means, for example, that if you consider yourself a democrat and you see democracy being attacked, you have to take it seriously and do your utmost to defend it. It also means that if you regard the European refugee policy as a scandalous piece of bigotry that makes a mockery both of the endlessly preached 'European values' and of the notion that lessons have been learned from German history, then you must campaign for an alternative refugee policy. And so on. There is no other way. The gap between the convenience of simply accepting things as they are and the effort of taking them seriously must not be allowed to get too big, otherwise people reach a point – and it happens quite quickly – when they no longer believe their own judgement. 'Live according to how you think, otherwise you will end up thinking according to how you live': such was the motto of the former president of Uruguay, José Mujica, known as El Pepe. Mujica was a member of the guerrilla group the Tupamaros, and spent 14 years of his life in prison. Later, as the elected president of Uruguay, he continued to live on a small farm, drove an old VW Beetle and kept just 10 per cent of his presidential salary on the basis that it was enough to live on. In an interview with the Austrian daily *Standard*, he summed up his political credo as follows: 'We want people to have more to eat, a roof over their heads, better health and education. Nothing beats life, and society comes a close second. Humans need to be part of a community. Anthropologically speaking, we are socialists.'

El Pepe treats the things that matter with political serious-ness but without taking himself too seriously.

I want my obituary to say:
He was willing to take things seriously – but not
too seriously

Another thing that needs to be taken seriously, by the way, is the game of skat. I can make this section quite short, as my fellow skat players A and S have already covered all the main points in a brilliant article.[5] Skat is an absolutely fascinating German card game in which you can still win even with a bad hand. And one where it is quite riveting to go on discussing afterwards what would have happened had you picked up the seven of clubs instead of the queen of clubs. This game only works if all players take it completely seriously for the duration of the game (which can be very long and alcohol fuelled). 'It's only a game' is a phrase that is only ever uttered by a person who knows absolutely nothing.

I want my obituary to say:
He was never quite as brilliant at skat as he thought he
was, but boy did he play a good game

And now, once again, for something completely different: in Germany, the search is on for a disposal site for nuclear waste. This search has been in progress for some time, and it has turned a whole region – the Wendland in the east, where the former salt mine of Gorleben was originally earmarked for the purpose – into a kind of Gallic village of resistance and sustainability initiatives. Ironically, when it came to the next screening for an appropriate site, Gorleben was eliminated in the first round, and so the search continues for a geologically suitable site that will be safe for a million years. In other words, one where nothing will happen to the layers of earth and rock over the next million years – where no water will penetrate and no one will take it into their head to dig up the buried material for the purposes of some act of galactic blackmail or similar. Just to be clear: somewhere where we'd rather nothing occurred for a million years, thank you very much.

There couldn't be a better way to illustrate the hubris of our generation. What kind of self-image does a culture have that dumps its waste on the next 40,000 generations? I say waste, but in the case of nuclear waste, this is a euphemism for stuff that is so incredibly dangerous that, if wrongly handled, it could trigger the end of humanity as soon as Generation 12,323. Or 564, or 4. Or 34,587.

Since there is a science for everything nowadays, complete with its own experts, the discipline of 'nuclear semiotics' has long wrestled with the question of how to warn the members of Generation 12,323 not to dig where the German radioactive waste management committee decided, 12,322 generations earlier, to sweep its legacy under the carpet. Because, in their wisdom, these boffins have realized that there's no absolute guarantee that we will still be able to order from Amazon, follow influencers and go on holiday to Mallorca in 300,000 years' time.

What's more, we don't even know for sure that people will still be using the same means of communication by then. So we are now faced with the Superman-style challenge of developing non-decaying kryptonite tablets, and the even more interest-ing one of writing something on them that future humans will be able to decipher and understand. You can make up your own mind whether to find this as amusing as a scene from *The Hitchhiker's Guide to the Galaxy* or so mind-blowingly stupid that you are forced to conclude, yet again, that humans are becoming steadily less intelligent over the course of evolution – indeed, ever since the Neolithic revolution.

Measured on the timescale of the nuclear waste question, that revolution was only yesterday, i.e., 13,000–14,000 years ago. That was when humans made the fatal mistake of aban-doning their nomadic hunter-gatherer lifestyle in favour of settling, cultivating plants, creating fields and storehouses, breeding animals, storing food supplies and bringing all those things into the world which – culminating in the likes of McDonald's – set the course for our subsequent retrogression.

Bear in mind here that *Homo sapiens* first appeared on the earth around 200,000 years ago, and it was some time before he began painting on cave walls – around 130,000 or 140,000 years ago in fact. Whether our fellow *sapiens* could

Fig. 3.5:   Warning sign for the year 243,077:
to gender or not to gender?

talk 60,000 years ago, and if so, how, we don't know. Despite all the achievements of paleoarchaeology, we really have no idea, as our ancestors unfortunately failed to leave behind any kryptonite tablets explaining in a form accessible to us what life was like for them and where they might have buried anything dodgy. And that's just 2,000 generations ago, not 40,000. Forty thousand generations ago there wasn't even such a thing as *Homo erectus*, and animals – luckily for them – had the place to themselves.

In short, the whole field of nuclear semiotics shows that scientific excellence and sheer stupidity are by no means mutually exclusive. To develop a technology and an accompanying meta-evolutionary guide for a future world that we imagine to be exactly the same as the present, only later in time – such a combination of naivety and hubris surely takes the biscuit. Do we really want to embarrass ourselves in the eyes of our Neanderthal ancestors and our Posthumanthal successors in x number of years' time? Do we want our own obituary to show us up as the dumbest cohort in the history of humanity?

No, of course not. The lesson we must learn from wrong-headed developments such as nuclear power is that all decisions must take into account the consequences for future generations and never restrict or block future development potential or opportunities for action. And certainly not for a million years. That is the minimum requirement for any civilization – something that modernity has yet to learn.

This basic insight can also be applied to climate policy. And it's exactly what Greta Thunberg, Luisa Neubauer and all other climate campaigners are calling for: intergenerational justice. Not to the absurd extent of 40,000 generations from now – all they are asking is that we don't deny today's Generation Z a future by doing little or nothing to protect the climate today. The continued disregard of global warming is, after all, not a phenomenon that can be analysed scientifically – it is a moral and political problem.

In his *Studies on the Germans*, Norbert Elias wrote that the 'restriction and expansion of opportunities for life and meaning in general and career opportunities in particular for the younger generations in a society' have a direct impact on the power balance between the generations, and that such 'processes lie at the heart of generational conflicts in society'.[6] For Elias, generational conflicts are in turn the strongest drivers of social dynamics – something that should not be romanticized: after all, national socialism was just as much a generational project as the Russian Revolution or the Arab Revolt, while

Elias's own observations were based on the example of the Baader–Meinhof Gang. The point is, any development that jeopardizes the next generation's future is deeply unfair, especially when the previous one is its main beneficiary. To put it graphically, my generation of baby boomers – which has seen a huge increase in material wealth thanks to a growth-based economy with no regard for the environmental consequences of its success – is like a fat globule floating in a soup that the younger generations will have to suck up. This cannot but lead to a call for intergenerational solidarity: the future must remain open, and that can only happen when older citizens begin to renounce their privileges over younger ones. The philosopher and popular science writer Richard David Precht has floated the bright idea of a year of compulsory volunteering for retirees, and another possibility would be to limit the upper age limit for voting. But, thinking more widely, such solidarity measures would have to include tax disincentives for activities harmful to the environment and climate, as well as a legal framework for sustainable business practices. Costly though this may be, it is the only just solution. What's more, considering how to change the way we do business, build, eat and live so that the price will no longer be paid by future generations could also unlock a good deal of creativity.

My original plan, incidentally, was to follow this 'obituary to myself' with an 'obituary to ourselves'. But I decided against it because, in my last book, *Alles könnte anders sein* ('Another World is Possible'), I had already outlined a mosaic of concrete utopias in which our lifestyles, economic systems and rules of civilization might, once again, produce a world fit for our grandchildren to live in. And on our platform FUTURZWEI, we have hundreds of examples – from businesswomen and start-ups to cooperatives, citizens' initiatives and much else besides – which show that it is possible not only to think beyond the status quo, but to take practical action.[7] To summarize these again here would be tedious. But all concrete utopias ultimately point to the same truth: the only way to secure our grandchildren's future is to refrain from making decisions that irreversibly limit the opportunities for development of generations to come.

I want my obituary to say:
He never took or supported decisions detrimental to the development of future generations

Intergenerational injustice is not always born of intent but, often enough, of stupidity. I have spent my life trying to fight stupidity – a vain enterprise, perhaps. The historian Lea Haller, who has written a brilliant essay on the history of stupidity,[8] believes it to be a historical constant which has neither increased nor decreased over time.

Furthermore, stupidity has nothing at all to do with either a lack of formal education or a lack of intelligence. There are intelligent professors and CEOs who are as thick as two short planks – they are incapable of making connections or synthesizing individual trains of thought into something new.

In Robert Musil's novel *The Man Without Qualities*, there is a character called Professor Hagauer, a teacher who is notable for his industriousness and respectability and whose 'fondness for florid neckties' is presumably an attempt to show that he is no common sort but a man willing to embrace the future.

> Such people can first be recognized for what they are even in their schooldays. They study not so much conscientiously – as it is called, confusing the effect with the cause – as in an orderly and practical fashion. They lay out every task beforehand, just as one has to lay out every piece of tomorrow's clothing, down to the last collar button, the night before if one wants to dress quickly and without a hitch in the morning. There is no chain of thought they cannot fix in their minds by using half a dozen such laid-out studs, and there is no denying that the results do

them credit and stand up to scrutiny. This takes them to the head of the class without their being perceived as prigs by their classmates.[9]

And they make their way in life with their five or ten mental shirt studs. You can go far professionally with such an approach – become head of the postal service or minister for education – yet still talk, or indeed enact, a lot of nonsense. Stupidity is, quantitatively speaking, a constant: by this measure, some 20 per cent of people are stupid. As long as that stupidity can't do any harm, it can even be rather endearing, but in the case of those whose role has the potential to inflict damage, it can have far-reaching consequences. Stupidity increases the probability of passive acceptance, failure to think for oneself, and susceptibility to crimes against humanity and ruptures of civilization. And group or indeed mass situations are bad for discernment and judgement but good for stupidity – what Sigmund Freud describes as the 'collective inhibition of intelligence' that occurs in the mass.

Stupidity also tends to be coupled with a contempt for all those who are too different to fit into the matrix of five or ten shirt studs. Nor is it a question of gender or 'left' or 'right' – such stupidity occurs across the genders (binary or non-binary) and in every shade of political opinion. A seasoned editor-in-chief of a political weekly once explained to me during a #MeToo discussion, after I remarked to her that men accounted for almost 90 per cent of the digital economy, and that this surely posed an urgent problem for gender policy: 'It may be true that more men are involved in developing the technology than women, but women use it just as much as men.' Need I say more?

This example is plucked at random from a million others and is fairly harmless, but stupidity can be very dangerous when coupled with power. In violent societies, this can produce a figure like the Nazi war criminal Adolf Eichmann and, in the milder conditions of a democratic constitutional state, someone like Richard Nixon. Conversely, intelligence has nothing to do with formal education, social standing, gender or ethnic origin. Georg Elser, who made a single-handed attempt on Hitler's life, had never been to university, and Stanislav Petrov, who saved humanity from nuclear destruction on 26 September 1983, was a lieutenant colonel, not an army general or commander-in-chief. Both had sounder judgement than the vast majority. The cultivation of autonomy and judgement must be encouraged and supported so that stupidity cannot win so easily and there are more people of the kind who make a difference.

However Sisyphean the task, there is a moral responsibility to take a stand against stupidity wherever it occurs. It is a hard and sometimes painful undertaking that is constantly threatened by the dark cloud of futility. But nevertheless . . .

I want my obituary to say:
He always tried to fight stupidity

One symptom of stupidity is the regurgitation of stupid words or phrases. It never ceases to amaze me how inane expressions – in English and German alike – turn into buzzwords that are suddenly on everyone's lips: 'if I'm honest', for instance, or 'it is what it is', 'at the end of the day', 'going forward', and many other phrases of the kind aptly described by the philosopher Harry Frankfurt as 'bullshit'. I always wonder why no one notices how utterly meaningless 'it is what it is' is: what else would it be? Another prime example of stupidity is when people talk about 'saving the world', or being 'a hero', or having the 'bravery' to do something useful for a change.

Once and for all: saving the world is not something within the power of the individual. Fact. Taking the bus does not make you a hero. Not even a climate hero. Fact. And you don't need bravery to do something in a democratic constitutional state. Fact. Bravery – while we're on the subject – is what you need to take to the streets in Belarus or Myanmar in the cause of freedom and democracy and at the risk of imprisonment, torture or death. Not in order to go on a demo or join an NGO in Germany: that is a folkloric exaggeration of simple democratic rights and duties. In his autobiographical account *Inside the War*, Otl Aicher, a friend of the White Rose resistance fighters Hans and Sophie Scholl, reflected on who and what can be considered brave under totalitarian rule and which individuals never have a monument erected to them, such as one 'humble village schoolteacher':

> Only someone who has lived in dark times can know what it means – what it perhaps means to someone personally – when a biology teacher stands up in front of a classroom, gives a brief introduction to the fundamentals of the natural sciences and then says, 'Biological substance is worthless as a subject matter. If I were to hold a National Socialist in one hand, and in the other a pile of faeces, the two would be – strictly biologically – one and the same.'[10]

An example of bravery is Myanmar's UN ambassador who, after the military coup in his country, makes a speech to the UN in which he denounces the crimes of the military and makes the three-finger sign of resistance adopted by the people of Myanmar. And an hour later finds himself out of a job and facing a future in which his life is constantly in danger. Other brave individuals include Edward Snowden, the Belarusian opposition leader Svetlana Tichanovskaja and the Chinese activist Howey Ou.

Those of us privileged enough to live in a free society only need to exercise bravery in order – at most – to dive from the 10-metre board at the local swimming pool, not in order to say what we think. Or to live according to the way we think. That's no big deal. Let's not flatter ourselves: it's perfectly normal and costs nothing.

I want my obituary to say:
He saw nothing wrong in saying what he thought

Finally, all this saving-the-world bullshit leads me on to another point that I should like to make in my obituary. All the self-promotion of the digital industry, particularly in its Silicon Valley variant, revolves around the tireless claim to be 'making the world a better place' (including every possible category of that 'world' that could conceivably be made 'better'). Amid this improvement drive, no one stops to ask whether the things being considered exclusively for their optimization potential should actually remain in the world, irrespective of whether they can be done better or worse with the aid of digitalization. A designer friend of mine, Julia Lohmann, asks the very good question: 'Do you want to keep this thing in your life?' Nowadays, this question always seems to come with the automatic answer: 'Yes, of course, if it exists, then I want it.' Or why else would people buy WLAN-enabled washing machines and fridges with digital content displays?

'Improvements' of this kind are surely not synonymous with progress. Of far greater relevance to the rational organization of society is the question of how to ensure a good life for all its members – such as by guaranteeing equality in terms of education and development opportunities, health and welfare, social security and participation. As such, it can sometimes make much more sense to abolish things than to improve them. In a society that aspires to offer equal access to mobility, for example, there is no point improving a mode of transport that is only used on an individual basis and which not everyone can afford – this does nothing to bring about a mobility system for all. On the contrary, private individual transport is a literal roadblock to the achievement of a public transport infrastructure that is digitally orchestrated in such a way as to guarantee an efficient and preferably free service for everyone. In other words, we don't need to improve the motor car, we need to get rid of it. The same goes for countless other things: a cruise ship cannot be optimized, because it is simply inappropriate. And the same goes for disposable barbecues, Alexa, facial recognition technology and all the rest of it: it has to go.

After all, many things are only in the world because someone saw a gap in the market or an opportunity to control it. Or, to put it more charitably, because – as in the case of the motor car – they are, socioculturally speaking, the product of a different age. But once these things have outlived their purpose, they cannot be improved. They don't need innovation but exnovation. How about a start-up whose business model is to rid the world of all the crap, for instance?

In order to decide whether something is a 'good' thing, we always need an independent variable: good for what? A particular use, an atmosphere, a social purpose, an increase in comfort or convenience, a pleasure? If this independent variable is not defined, we end up with cars that are so incomprehensibly large, heavy and ugly that technology historians in a hundred years' time will be at a loss to explain why such things existed – particularly at a time of such strain on the environment and resources. They exist because the question of 'good for what?' was never asked; the only goal was 'better'. And that 'better' has a lot to answer for.

In my view, the 'good for what?' is by no means only a functional category, however: it can apply just as well to all sorts of non-functional things, such as the performance of a piece of music or a play – anything, in fact, that can be defined as a cultural product. That could be a garden, a meal, a wine, sex, a story or anything else that requires an added element of 'goodness' beyond the purely functional in order to qualify as good.

Then there is, inevitably, the equally problematic yet essential category of the beautiful, which is urgently in need of review. There is no beauty in getting tips from Alexa on where to buy something cheaply, and there is no beauty in the fact that children can't play in the street – even if the cars are all electric and energy efficient, they still monopolize the space. Nor is there beauty in houses made of money or the restoration of palaces from sheer lack of imagination (another thing that will have future historians scratching their heads).

There can be beauty in environments where one is undisturbed by unwanted things, algorithms, noise and emissions, and there may be beauty in neighbourhoods where people feel so at home that they live in harmony with each other and the things around them. In other words, the creation of beauty is not a technical but a social task. We must regain the confidence to use such terms in our work; to encounter the world as it is, or what Hartmut Rosa calls the 'uncontrollable'. That doesn't mean that the results of our work have to be agreeable to all, or standardizable, or universally valid. On the contrary: only things that are worth arguing over can be good. You can't argue about the bad stuff. Or as the abstract artist Gerhard Richter once said, 'Creating the incomprehensible has absolutely nothing to do with turning out any old bunkum, because bunkum is always comprehensible.'[11]

I want my obituary to say:
He was always susceptible to beauty

A sentiment, incidentally, that is expressed in the poem 'Avenidas' by the Swiss-Bolivian poet Eugen Gomringer. The poem – a hymn to the beauty of flowers and women – was painted in large lettering on the wall of a Berlin college but was condemned as sexist by a student body with the 'five-to-ten-shirt-stud' mentality in league with an equally stupid

Fig. 3.6:   Not just scenery: the Peesten dance linden

college management, who ordered it to be painted over (so short, I might add, is the path to fascism – but that's another story).

And so to another story about beauty. Something that moved me very much during the past year was a visit to a dance linden. Yes, you heard right: a dance linden. Some time ago I was invited to a lecture by the Upper Franconia IT Cluster, and on the way to Bamberg station, the organizer, an affable man named Hans Ulrich Gruber, offered to show me the dance linden in the nearby village of Peesten.

For some reason Mr Gruber must have guessed I'd be fascinated by the dance linden. As indeed I was. Normally, you would dance *under* a tree. But in the case of a dance linden, you dance *in* it. These trees are planted so that, when they reach a suitable size, a dance floor can be built in the branches for the purpose of village celebrations. The few dance lindens still in existence are very old. The one in Peesten, which I gazed upon open mouthed, was originally planted between 1550 and 1600,

and is described in a report from the mid-nineteenth century
as follows:

> Built on the spreading branches is an 87 m² dance hall which
> is reached by a stone spiral staircase with twenty-two steps
> and an iron balustrade. The floor of this hall is covered with
> oakwood tiles. The walls are also in green-painted oak, and the
> branches grow towards them, forming a dense wall of foliage.
> The dance hall is entered via a wide door. Eleven windows, each
> measuring 90 cm wide by 120 cm high, afford an open view to
> the charming surrounding landscape and the Main valley.[12]

Of course, such a tree has to be maintained and replaced
when necessary, but all the same: here we have something
that has existed for five or six centuries for the sole purpose of
enabling local people to celebrate special occasions by dancing
among its branches. That strikes me as a beautiful symbol of
how, as a society, we can cultivate a peaceful relationship with
nature – a relationship that is strongly associated with joy and
beauty. And that's the key: we need to develop non-destructive
modes of interaction with the natural world we depend on,
reaping its fruits not in a warlike fashion but in a peaceful one
that leaves no devastation behind. Earlier, I quoted Eva von
Redecker's observation: 'Perhaps our fundamental mistake is
seeing nature as a backdrop.' The dance linden is not a backdrop: the way people use it is to get right inside it.

If we pursue this line of thinking, perhaps we will find a way
out of the disastrous instrumental rationality of the modern
age, which views the world exclusively as something to be used
for other purposes. Supposing we planted lots more trees in
towns and cities to improve CO_2 absorption. One tree – one
purpose: CO_2 reduction. Fine, we can do that.

But now imagine if our reason for planting trees in the city
were an aesthetic one – one that grants the tree a value in
and of itself: then a whole different set of social consequences

would follow. Just as people can dance in the dance linden, so they could picnic or read under the municipal tree; lovers could even carve hearts in it with their initials. Then the trees would not be just background, not 'for' something, but integral to our very existence. Their ability to absorb greenhouse gases would be a welcome collateral benefit, but the primary purpose would be to build a new relationship with nature. And that's exactly what is needed: a transformation of our lifeworld that enables us to live a good life not by ignoring our natural environment but by interacting with it in a whole new way. Not smart cities, but good cities. And this is – as the dance linden demonstrates – not a scientific project or a reactive one devised in order to solve a problem. Rather, it is a proactive attempt to design and implement better ways of life. A dance linden is a good thing irrespective of climate change. We must pursue and enact ideas and visions that would still be desirable even if there were no such thing as biodiversity loss or marine pollution or rainforest destruction. In short, we make life far too easy for ourselves if we only act when external pressures leave us no other option. Even without those pressures, there is still every reason to do things better than at present.

In this sense, perhaps the dance linden is a right answer to the wrong question. Because our current response to the challenges posed by the destruction of the very resources we depend on is based on the wrong questions: it seeks to optimize, instead of abandoning the wrong path, to continue instead of stopping, to create more instead of less. These are all routine responses to wrongly framed questions, such as: How do we make cars 'climate neutral'? Answer: by electrifying them. Which technology will allow us to go on increasing our energy consumption while remaining 'climate neutral'? Answer: renewables. How do we 'decarbonize' the global economy and its growth? Answer: by magic. The right questions are: How will we get around? How much energy do we need for any given lifestyle? What kind of economy will further our project to guarantee a good life for all?

My questions relate to our cultural model: how do we want to live? How do we continue to build our civilization project? How do we guarantee freedom? Asking questions like this puts technology in the place where it belongs: it helps us formulate an answer, but it can never be the answer in itself. That's not being anti-technology, but pro-humanity.

I want my obituary to say:
He considered the right questions more important than
the wrong answers

And now to the most difficult part. Only those who fear life are afraid of death. I was originally going to put this phrase – which I recently happened to catch in a film and instantly jotted down – at the end of this book. But then I asked myself whether I could really endorse that sentiment and was sadly forced to admit: no, I am still afraid of death. But does that make me fear life? Writing this book has done a great deal to lessen my fear of death. In fact, the whole project was prompted by my recognition of the fact that I will die one day, whether tomorrow, or in 30 years, or some time in between. But one point that came up time and time again in my discussions about stopping was that it is not a natural thing for humans to do: it has to be learned and practised. And therefore we must apply ourselves calmly to the business of learning not to be afraid of death. Another point was that time is not really the right category for measuring life: when it comes to the meaning of life, it doesn't matter how long it lasts. We must free ourselves from the notion that a person's life is 'too short', or that they have died 'too soon'. The meaning of a 'hazarded' life, to use Johannes Heimrath's expression, does not depend on its duration. We only think so by way of compensation – a kind of avoidance manoeuvre – because modernity confronts us with the wild, private form of death to which every individual must submit – and that is something which, understandably enough, we want to postpone as long as possible. It is only thus that the category of duration comes into play, as a logical consequence of fear. If, as Wittgenstein says, the 'solution to the riddle of life in space and time . . . lies outside space and time', then there is something deeply conciliatory in that since we will never be able to solve the riddle. Not as long as we live. To misquote the abstract artist Ad Reinhardt, life is life and everything else is everything else.

I want my obituary to say:
He learnt not to be afraid of death

Well, almost.

IV

An Immense Journey

Doesn't the whole poetry of human existence reside in the fact that we are all destined to die? And, before that, to have lived? And that, in the end, there are no differences between us: no one is so privileged as to be exempt from the reality of death. Were it otherwise, there would be no sense of wrong, no fight for justice, no civilizing process. It is only because we are mortal that we can be good.

And how does Franz Kafka's story 'The Departure' continue? Like this:

'You have no provisions with you', he said. 'I need none', I said. 'The journey is so long that I must die of hunger if I don't get anything on the way. No provisions can save me. For it is, fortunately, a truly immense journey.'

Twelve maxims for answering the question: What do I want my legacy to be?
- Life has taken a chance on me.
- The space for change is within, not outside, our limits.
- The time for change is the present, not the future.
- Targets are not actions.
- Stopping needs a reason, but the ability to stop takes skill.

- Stopping cements an achievement; continuing banalizes it.
- Dogma gets you nowhere.
- Nor do subjunctives.
- The word 'actually' should be avoided.
- The meaning of a life does not depend on its duration.
- You must think about the conclusion before you reach the end.
- There is life before death. And *only* before.

Notes

Chapter I Away from Here

1 *Frankfurter Allgemeine Zeitung*, 11 December 2020, 6.

2 Jared Diamond, *Collapse: How Societies Choose to Fail or Succeed*, New York: Viking Press, 2005.

3 Harald Welzer, *Climate Wars: What People Will Be Killed For in the 21st Century*, trans. Patrick Camiller, Cambridge: Polity, 2012.

4 This idea is explored in Cormac McCarthy's novel *The Road*.

5 Central to the argument for a 2- or 1.5-degree target is the possibility that, if these values are exceeded, this will lead to irreversible dynamics with mutually reinforcing consequences – a point made particularly starkly by T. M. Lenton et al. (2019) in their agenda-setting article 'Climate Tipping Points – Too Risky to Bet Against': 'We argue that the intervention time left to prevent tipping could already have shrunk towards zero, whereas the reaction time to achieve net zero emissions is 30 years at best. Hence we might already have lost control of whether tipping happens.' (https://www.nature.com/articles/d41586-019-03595 -0)

6 In an interview, one of the world's leading climate scientists, Stefan Rahmstorf, warns:

At 1.7 or 1.8 degrees, we will already lose the majority of the world's coral reefs; at 2 degrees we will lose them all. Half of the Great Barrier Reef in Australia has been wiped out in recent years. These natural wonders are already dying. Another problem is the loss of the great ice shields, notably in Greenland. There is a tipping point at which the melting of Greenland's ice becomes unstoppable. But we don't know exactly what that is. With every tenth of a degree we go above 1.5 degrees the risk grows that we will exceed it, and that island states and coastal cities will eventually have to be abandoned. If warming continues above 1.5 degrees, the world won't end with a big bang, as some activists imagine. But we are constantly running into ever greater risks and will lose more and more – biodiversity, ecosystems, food security – with every tenth of a degree we go above 1.5 degrees.

(https://www.rnd.de/politik/klimaforscher-rahmstorf-wir-mus sen-mehr-uber-losungen-diskutieren-7K3YKDQF4FEBZMTV USJSCZNPIE.html)

7 Eva Horn, 'Der erhellende Blitz der Katastrophe: Die Welt ohne Menschen', *Aviso* 2, 2017, 24–31.
8 https://de.statista.com/statistik/daten/studie/185394/umfrage /entwicklung-der-lebenserwartung-nach-geschlecht/
9 Steven Pinker, *The Better Angels of Our Nature: Why Violence Has Declined*, New York: Viking, 2011.
10 Quoted in Franz Mehring, *Karl Marx: The Story of His Life*, ch. 9.3, trans. Edward Fitzgerald (available in Marxists Internet Library, https://www.marxists.org/archive/mehring/1918/marx /ch09.htm)
11 Philippe Ariès, *The Hour of Our Death*, trans. Helen Weaver, New York: Alfred A. Knopf, 1981.
12 Ibid., 119.
13 Peter L. Berger and Thomas Luckmann, *The Social Construction of Reality: A Treatise in the Sociology of Knowledge*, New York: Anchor Books, 1966, 101.

14 Ibid., 120.

15 Ariès, *The Hour of Our Death*, 358.

16 Peter Sloterdijk, *Making the Heavens Speak: Religion as Poetry*, trans. Robert P. Hughes, Cambridge: Polity, 2022.

17 Armin Nassehi and Georg Weber, *Tod, Modernität und Gesellschaft. Entwurf einer Theorie der Todesverdrängung*, Wiesbaden: VS, 1989, here esp. 113–55.

18 Max Horkheimer and Theodor W. Adorno, *Dialectic of Enlightenment*, trans. Edmund Jephcott, Stanford: Stanford University Press, 2002, 9.

19 Norbert Elias, *The Loneliness of the Dying*, trans. Edmund Jephcott, New York/London: Continuum, 1985, 28.

20 Uwe Volkmann, 'Gras im Wind?' *Frankfurter Allgemeine Zeitung*, 6 April 2021, 7.

21 Ironically, this programme was used by a writer with the Swiss daily *Neue Zürcher Zeitung* as the basis for an extended piece on the different levels of professionalism in home recordings during the pandemic. I was cited as an example of an academic media expert who rose to the media challenge with supreme technical skill, using a professional lighting, camera and sound system. Media expert, my foot! My entire arsenal consisted (and still consists) of a seven-year-old MacBook Air and, as for myself, I was minutes away from a heart attack!

22 Leo Tolstoy, *The Death of Ivan Ilyich*, trans. Louise and Aylmer Maude, in Michael R. Katz (ed.), *Tolstoy's Short Fiction*, New York/London: W. W. Norton, 2008, 84.

23 Sloterdijk, *Making the Heavens Speak*, 72.

24 That is, unless it is introduced – in circumstances such as a pandemic – as a substantiated and temporary exceptional measure, which can only be extended by a parliamentary vote.

25 Michael Kopatz, *Schluss mit der Ökomoral! Wie wir die Welt retten, ohne ständig daran zu denken*, Munich: oekom 2019, 27.

26 The following paragraphs are revised versions of a text entitled 'Wissen wird überbewertet' ('Knowledge is overrated'), published

by de Gruyter in the supplement to the 23 August 2021 issue of the *Berliner Theologische Zeitschrift*.

27 Raj Patel and Jason W. Moore, *A History of the World in Seven Cheap Things: A Guide to Capitalism, Nature and the Future of the Planet*, Oakland: University of California Press, 2020. (See also https://jasonwmoore.com/wp-content/uploads/2018/05/Pa tel-and-Moore-How-the-chicken-nugget-became-the-true-sym bol-of-our-era-2018-Guardian.pdf)

28 Ibid. In February 2021, Germany passed the Supply Chain Act, which marks a first step towards tackling institutional irresponsibility within supply chains by making German companies (initially large corporations) liable for abuses on the part of their suppliers, such as the use of child labour or non-compliance with health and safety standards.

29 Ivan Illich, *Tools for Conviviality*, New York: Harper & Row, 1973, 94.

30 Ernst Bloch, *Experimentum Mundi*, vol. 15, Frankfurt: Suhrkamp, 1977, 237.

31 Ibid., 231.

32 Ibid., 235.

33 Harald Welzer, *Täter. Wie aus ganz normalen Menschen Massenmörder werden*, Frankfurt: Fischer, 2005.

34 The following reflections are a revised version of extracts from Harald Welzer, *Mental Infrastructures: How Growth Entered the World and Our Souls*, Berlin: Heinrich Böll Foundation, 2011.

35 Martin Kohli, 'Normalbiographie und Individualität: Zur institutionellen Dynamik des gegenwärtigen Lebenslauf regimes', in Hanns-Georg Brose and Bruno Hildenbrand (eds), *Vom Ende des Individuums zur Individualität ohne Ende*, Opladen: Westdeutscher Verlag, 1988, 35.

36 Hanns-Georg Brose and Bruno Hildenbrand (eds), *Vom Ende des Individuums zur Individualität ohne Ende*, Opladen: Westdeutscher Verlag, 13.

37 Joseph Vogl, *Kalkül und Leidenschaft. Poetik des ökonomischen Menschen*, Zürich: diaphanes, 2009.

38 Ibid.

39 Vogl, *Kalkül und Leidenschaft*, 336.

40 Wolfgang Schivelbusch, *The Railway Journey: The Industrialization of Time and Space in the Nineteenth Century*, Berkeley: University of California Press, 1986.

41 UllrichWolfgang, *Habenwollen. Wie funktioniert die Konsumkultur*, Frankfurt: Fischer, 2006.

42 Jürgen Osterhammel, *The Transformation of the World: A Global History of the Nineteenth Century*, trans. Patrick Camiller, Princeton: Princeton University Press, 2014, 657.

43 Ibid., 657–8.

44 Jean Laplanche and Jean-Bertrand Pontalis, *The Language of Psychoanalysis*, trans. Donald Nicholson-Smith, London: Hogarth Press, 1973.

45 Michael Hagner, *Der Hauslehrer. Die Geschichte eines Kriminalfalls*, Frankfurt: Suhrkamp, 2010.

46 Osterhammel, *The Transformation of the World*.

47 Welzer, *Mental Infrastructures*.

48 Horkheimer and Adorno, *Dialectic of Enlightenment*, 1.

49 Ibid., 6.

50 Eva von Redecker, *Revolution für das Leben. Philosophie der neuen Protestformen*, Frankfurt: Fischer 2020, 115.

51 Karl Marx, *Capital* (vol. 1), London: Penguin, 1976, 637–8.

52 Horkheimer and Adorno, *Dialectic of Enlightenment*, 19.

53 Ibid., 25.

54 Ludwig Wittgenstein, *Tractatus Logico-philosophicus*, 6.341, trans. Charles Kay Ogden, London: Routledge & Kegan Paul, 1922.

55 Ludger Heidbrink, 'Ambivalenzen des Finalismus', unpublished lecture manuscript, 2004, 8.

56 Horn, 'Der erhellende Blitz der Katastrophe'.

57 Roger Willemsen, *Who We Were*, Frankfurt: Fischer, 2016 [SH: partial translation by Simon Pare available at: https://bilder -fischer.s3.eu-central-1.amazonaws.com/sampletranslations/97 83103972856_english_translation.pdf]

58 Ibid.

59 Ibid., 31. [SH: my translation]

60 Bradd Shore, *Culture in Mind: Cognition, Culture, and the Problem of Meaning*, Oxford: Oxford University Press, 1996.

61 Gerald Hüther, Lothar Adler and Eckart Rüther, 'Die neurobiologische Verankerung psychosozialer Erfahrungen', *Zeitschrift für psychosomatische Medizin* 45, 1999, 2–17.

62 Michael Tomasello, *Becoming Human: A Theory of Ontogeny*, Cambridge, MA/London: Harvard University Press, 2019, 34.

63 Hans-J. Markowitsch and Harald Welzer, *The Development of Autobiographical Memory*, London: Psychology Press, 2009.

64 Tomasello, *Becoming Human*, 21.

65 Carel van Schaik and Karin Isler, 'Gehirne, Lebensverläufe und die Evolution des Menschen', in Ernst-Peter Fischer and Klaus Wiegandt (eds), *Evolution und Kultur des Menschen*, Frankfurt: Fischer, 2010, 143f.

66 Friedemann Schrenk, 'Menschwerdung I: Die Auskunft der Fossilien', in Ernst-Peter Fischer and Klaus Wiegandt (eds), *Evolution und Kultur des Menschen*, Frankfurt: Fischer, 2010, 47.

67 Tomasello, *Becoming Human*, 153.

68 Hannah Arendt, *The Human Condition*, Chicago: University of Chicago Press, 1958, 237.

69 Ibid., 237.

70 Ibid., 245.

71 Arendt, too, uses this expression to refer to the classical separation of nature and humanity, but it is irrelevant to the argument here.

72 Ibid., 246.

73 Ibid., 247.

74 Ibid.

Chapter II Narratives of Stopping – and of Life

1 https://www.deutschlandfunkkultur.de/tino-sehgal-imberlinergropius-bau-kunst-die-nicht-von.1013.de.html?dram:article_id=323682

2 https://taz.de/!598519/

3 The following account is a co-production of realities:united and myself, a previous version of which appeared in the volume *Imagineering*, published by Jörg Metelmann and myself (see Jörg Metelmann and Harald Welzer (eds), *Imagineering. Wie Zukunft gemacht wird*, Frankfurt: Fischer, 2020, 145ff.).

4 Arendt, *The Human Condition*, 246.

5 https://www.spiegel.de/psychologie/christiane-zu-salmim-por sche-heult-man-nicht-a-c65f57d1-9e25-4ae5-89dd-57011b47 9671

6 Christiane zu Salm, *Dieser Mensch war ich. Nachrufe auf das eigene Leben*, Munich: Goldmann, 2013.

7 Barney G. Glaser and Anselm Strauss, *Awareness of Dying*, Chicago: Aldine, 1965.

8 Thomas Macho, *Das Leben nehmen. Suizid in der Moderne*, Frankfurt: Suhrkamp, 2018.

9 Hans-Dietrich Reckhaus, *Why Every Fly Counts: Value and Endangerment of Insects*, Cham: Springer International Publishing, 2017.

Chapter III An Obituary to the Rest of My Life

1 Karl E. Weick and Kathleen M. Sutcliffe, *Managing the Unexpected: Resilient Performance in an Age of Uncertainty*, New York: Wiley, 2007.

2 Hannah Arendt, *Origins of Totalitarianism*, Part Three, San Diego: Harcourt, 1968.

3 *The Goebbels Diaries, 1940–41*, ed. Fred Taylor, London: Hamish Hamilton, 1982.

4 Arendt, *Origins of Totalitarianism*, Part Three, 48ff.

5 Andre Wilkens and Stephan Wegner, 'Der Spieler. Wie man mit Skat die Welt verstehen kann', in Dana Giesecke, Hans-Georg Soeffner and Klaus Wiegandt (eds), *Welzers Welt. Störungen im Betriebsablauf*, Frankfurt: Fischer, 2018, 437–43.

6 Norbert Elias, *Studien über die Deutschen*, Frankfurt: Suhrkamp, 1989, 320.

7 www.futurzwei.org

8 https://www.nzz.ch/geschichte/die-vielen-gesichter-derdummh
   eit-ld.1608417

9 Robert Musil, *The Man Without Qualities*, trans. Sophie Wilkins,
   London: Picador, 2017, 512.

10 Otl Aicher, *Inside the War*, quoted in translation in Ruth Sachs,
   White Rose History, vol. 1 (academic version): *Coming Together*
   (31 January 1933–30 April 1942), ch. 9, 4.

11 Hans Ulrich Obrist and Dietmar Elger (eds), *Gerhard Richter:
   Text, Writings, Interviews and Letters 1961–2007*, London:
   Thames & Hudson, 2009, 20.

12 http://www.tanzlinde-peesten.de/de/tanzlinde/historische-tanz
   linde/

Index

Page numbers in *italics* denote an illustration